THEATRE C

Phelim McDermott & Lee Simpson

THEATRE OF BLOOD

OBERON BOOKS
LONDON

WWW.OBERONBOOKS.COM

First published in 2005 by Oberon Books Ltd
521 Caledonian Road, London N7 9RH
Tel: +44 (0) 20 7607 3637 / Fax: +44 (0) 20 7607 3629
e-mail: info@oberonbooks.com
www.oberonbooks.com

A catalogue record for this book is available from the British
Library.

PB ISBN: 9781840025781

Authors' Notes

This adaptation of *Theatre of Blood* makes liberal use of dialogue from the plays of William Shakespeare. Mostly these quotes are verbatim, but sometimes they have been paraphrased to fit the context in which they are used. We therefore owe Shakespeare our thanks for providing these unparalleled riches for us to plunder, and our apologies for butchering it to suit our own purposes.

The very early conversations about how we might tackle this project were between Phelim, myself and Julian Crouch (the other artistic director of Improbable). Next, the fundamental decisions about how our version would differ from the film were reached through discussions between Phelim and myself. I then took on the job of translating our discussions into something that resembled a script. At various points during that process Phelim would respond to what I'd done and those ideas would help to shape the development of the piece. Once the design and rehearsal process began, the development of the script became subject once again to ongoing discussions between Phelim and myself.

There have of course been other people who have helped us get this far, and our special thanks go to:

Simon Russell Beale who provided an invaluable insight into the themes and ideas that run through the entire Shakespearean cannon, as well as a sense of what it is that makes Shakespeare so unique for many actors.

Stella McDermott who guided me to some very useful Shakespearean texts when I had not a clue where to start.

Lyn Gardner and Paul Taylor who provided fascinating information about the life of a theatre critic.

Nick Hytner, Jack Bradley, Julian Crouch, Tom Morris and Shelley Silas who all offered excellent feedback on the script at various stages in its development.

Our brilliant cast and stage management team, who have suggested cuts and emendations to make the thing work better on a stage.

If I have forgotten to give anyone due credit my only excuse is that this page is being written in a great deal of haste in the midst of what might be called 'the rehearsal tunnel' and ask you to castigate me in person for my lapse.

This is the script as it exists two weeks before we present the first preview to the public. There will be many alterations between now and then, and indeed many more once that most useful of factors, audience feedback, has its say.

Lee Simpson

*

I first saw *Theatre Of Blood* when I was a teenager on late night Friday television. At the time it was a perfect combination for me: a horror film about the theatre. It is story of a grand actor who is so wounded by bad reviews that he becomes murderous. It has a wonderful central performance by Vincent Price, which is tinged with the faint air of recrimination that in his career we had never quite taken him seriously. He plays the Shakespeare marvellously and although a camp film, his performance never is. There is at the heart of the film something quite touching which we hope to capture in our own version.

I had often thought it would make a great basis for a theatre show. The original screenplay by Anthony Greville-Bell, with its fantastic ideas for each Shakespearean death, cries out to be put onto a stage. Though we were not quite aware of the puzzle we had set ourselves in taking it from screen to stage.

If our show is in any way as memorable as this remarkable film, then we will be very content.

We have Nicholas Hytner, director of the National Theatre, to thank for his insistence that we do the show in the Lyttelton; if this had not happened then we would not have got interested in the story of the National Theatre building and it would not have its own particular place in our adaptation.

Phelim McDermott

For further information about Improbable and our productions please visit **www.improbable.co.uk**

For further information about The National Theatre and its productions please visit **www.nationaltheatre.org.uk**

Dramatis Personæ

The Critics

PETER DEVLIN
The Times

GEORGE MAXWELL
The Daily Telegraph

MICHAEL MERRIDEW
The Sunday Times

SALLY PATTERSON
The Guardian

CHLOË MOON
The Observer

TREVOR DICKENS
The Evening Standard

OLIVER LARDING
The Daily Mail

EDWARD LIONHEART
An Actor

MIRANDA LIONHEART
His Daughter

A CHORUS
of Six Tramps

Improbable's version of *Theatre of Blood* was first performed at the National Theatre (Lyttelton) London on 9 May 2005, with the following cast:

EDWARD LIONHEART, Jim Broadbent

MIRANDA LIONHEART, Rachael Stirling

PETER DEVLIN, Mark Lockyer

GEORGE MAXWELL, Paul Bentall

MICHAEL MERRIDEW, Bette Bourne

SALLY PATTERSON, Hayley Carmichael

CHLOË MOON, Sally Dexter

TREVOR DICKENS, Steve Steen

OLIVER LARDING, Tim McMullan

A CHORUS OF TRAMPS,
Gerard Bell, Stephen Harper, Nick Haverson,
Rachael Spence, Victoria Willing, Edward Woodall

Director Phelim McDermott

Designer Rae Smith

Associate Director Lee Simpson

Lighting Designer Colin Grenfell

Music Joby Talbot (published by Chester Music Ltd)

Illusionist Paul Kieve

Fight Director Terry King

Sound Designer Gareth Fry

Prologue

An empty theatre. Old, unloved and dilapidated. Almost derelict.

Silence.

A flash of lightning and a crash of thunder herald a violent storm inside the building.

Each crack of lightning illuminates images of the great actors of history in moments of Shakespearean acting in the grand style. The kind of acting you just don't see any more. Declamatory, ridiculous, magnificent. An orgy of beautiful over-acting.

Towering above the stage we become aware of a cloaked figure. His outstretched arms seem to encompass the whole building.

LIONHEART: Know thus far forth.
    By accident most strange, bountiful Fortune,
    Now my dear lady, hath mine enemies
    Brought to this shore; and by my prescience
    I find my zenith doth depend upon
    A most auspicious star, whose influence
    If now I court not but omit, my fortunes
    Will ever after droop.

The cloaked figure and the old style actors disappear back into the shadows.

The storm now sounds as if it is outside the building and moving into the distance.

The stage is once again empty and dark.

Scene 1

In a far corner of the stage a door gently opens. A man stands silhouetted in the door frame for a second or two. He closes the door softly behind him and makes his way to the centre of the stage.

He is in his mid-thirties. Dressed in contemporary but not overly trendy clothes for 1973. This is PETER DEVLIN.

He stands there for a moment. Interested by the feeling of being centre stage in a large empty theatre.

Another door swings open. An older man appears. Grey haired, suited and carrying a brolly. Old school. He is a man clearly unaffected by the atmosphere of the old theatre. This is GEORGE MAXWELL.

MAXWELL: Hello?

DEVLIN: Hello.

MAXWELL strides onto the stage allowing the door to slam behind him. As he gets closer he recognises DEVLIN.

MAXWELL: Devlin.

DEVLIN: Hello George.

MAXWELL: What's going on?

DEVLIN: I've no idea.

MAXWELL: What?

DEVLIN: I've no idea.

MAXWELL: No idea?

DEVLIN: No.

MAXWELL produces a letter.

MAXWELL: But I received this, asking me to come along here this evening, and when I saw you standing there I naturally thought…oh.

DEVLIN has a letter too.

What's going on?…sorry…

DEVLIN: I've seen it from the outside but never been in.

MAXWELL: It was boarded up before your time.

DEVLIN: Did you see anything here?

MAXWELL: What? Oh yes. Did you read my review today?

DEVLIN: Erm…

MAXWELL: Of the Feydeau?

DEVLIN: No. I don't think I…

MAXWELL: Do you know what the bloody editor cut out of it? The best line. The best bloody line!

DEVLIN: Really? What was that?

MAXWELL: I said that Juliette McGowan attacked the role of Madame Chandebise with both hands…and strangled it to death. I mean if one can't be provocative what's the point? What's the point? I've a good mind to resign. Now that would cause merry hell if they lost me…I've had approaches you know…oh yes…

Both turn to the sound of conversation as voices are heard approaching.

From the wings a man and a woman appear.

He is a well rounded figure, but very dapper, if not a little flamboyant in his dress. In his early fifties. He is carrying two small dogs. This is MICHAEL MERRIDEW.

She is younger. Thirty-ish. Not unfashionably dressed but wearing an outfit that makes it clear she is not attempting to be alluring to either sex in any way. She is carrying a copy of the letter we have seen MAXWELL and DEVLIN produce. This is SALLY PATTERSON.

MERRIDEW: Good God! It's a critics convention!

PATTERSON: I said I'd heard someone.

MERRIDEW: (*Indicating his dogs.*) Cecily and Gwendolen are intrigued as to why we have been gathered here, aren't you my little dumplings?

MAXWELL: Exactly. What's going on?

PATTERSON: Did you send this?

DEVLIN: Why do people think it's me? I received one same as George.

MERRIDEW: You have the appropriate spirit of mischief my dear boy, (*To the dogs.*) doesn't he girls?

PATTERSON: Well I hope that whoever it is, gets on with whatever it is pretty soon (*Referring to the letter.*) 'March 15th – nine o'clock.' I have got better things to do.

MAXWELL: Perhaps it meant nine o'clock in the morning.

MERRIDEW: Do be sensible George, who would ask a theatre critic to be anywhere at nine o'clock in the morning?

MAXWELL: Good point. Did either of you read my review today? Do you know what the bloody editor cut out of it?

A voice from the auditorium.

MOON: George you are such an idiot. Even if we had read it, which most of us have but none of us will admit to, how could we know what was not in it?

Climbing up the treads onto the stage from the auditorium are three more people.

The first is an elegantly dressed, mature and sexy woman. This is CHLOË MOON.

Next up is a rakishly attired middle-aged man who may or may not be wearing a toupee. This is TREVOR DICKENS.

The last onto the stage is a slightly shambolic figure, totally unconcerned with his appearance. This is OLIVER LARDING.

PATTERSON: Have you been there all along?

MAXWELL: What is going on?

DICKENS: Heard every word.

MOON: Some of them anyway, really my dears – Diction! Projection!

LARDING: I wouldn't advise you to chuck away your notebooks and venture over the footlights just yet.

MERRIDEW: The gang's all here.

PATTERSON: You just sat out there and watched us?

DICKENS: That is what we do for a living dear.

PATTERSON: I am not your 'dear'.

DICKENS: Thank goodness for that!

PATTERSON: For once I agree with you.

LARDING: We all got letters too.

MOON: But they each promise something different.

MERRIDEW: Really?

LARDING: Take a look.

Some of them do.

DEVLIN: Mine simply invites me to see the theatre. Says it might be an early unattributed Frank Matcham. I'm pretty sure it isn't.

MERRIDEW: Ours is far more thrilling isn't it Cecily? 'Your carriage awaits your pleasure.' And do you know, at the very moment I was reading it I heard a toot on a car horn, and outside my door was a black cab with the passenger door open. I have a weakness for cars with the passenger door open.

MOON: I thought mine was from Al.

DEVLIN: Alan Finchley?

MOON: It's the sort of thing Al would do. Empty theatre. Might get caught.

PATTERSON: How can you…carry on with an actor you might have to review?

MAXWELL: Carry on with an actor. I don't think I've seen that one. Was Sid James in it?

PATTERSON: Don't you think you might be abusing your position?

MOON: What's the point in having leverage if you don't pull the lever every now and again?

LARDING: Mine asked if I was interested in a half case of Château Margaux '61.

DICKENS: Without the irritating inconvenience of import duty or indeed establishing whether you were buying from the rightful owner I assume?

LARDING: All's fair in love and wine. Sally?

PATTERSON: I was following a lead.

MAXWELL: Theatre critics don't follow leads, they write about them. Juvenile leads. Leading actors. Do you see?

PATTERSON: Some of us would like to address more pressing journalistic issues than 'what I thought about the play I saw last night'.

LARDING: Looking for a headline instead of a byline?

DEVLIN: Trevor?

DICKENS: I was asked along to offer some advice to a theatre group.

A student theatre group.

From the letter she seemed keen.

MERRIDEW: How philanthropic of you.

DICKENS: What about you George?

MAXWELL: Oh! er…erm.

MOON: Come on George, we've all spilled our guts.

PATTERSON: Charming.

LARDING: It wouldn't have anything to do with this approach?

MERRIDEW: Approach?

MOON: George has been approached.

MERRIDEW: Lucky George.

MOON: He said so before you came in. 'I've had approaches,' he said.

MAXWELL: If you must know I was asked here to discuss the possibility of a post at the National Theatre.

LARDING: The Old Vic?

MAXWELL: At the new South Bank.

MOON: If they ever finish building the bloody thing.

MERRIDEW: What sort of post?

MAXWELL: Literary manager. Advising the artistic director. Selecting the repertoire. That sort of thing.

The possibility that one of their number might get such a post rather takes the wind out of their sails.

DEVLIN: The gang's all here.

MERRIDEW: I think I've already noted that dear boy.

DEVLIN: The gang which decided the Critics' Circle Award for Shakespeare 1972.

LARDING: Yes he's right. This is the entire panel for last year's award.

MAXWELL: It still doesn't explain…what's going on.

PATTERSON: I don't care what's going on. Whoever arranged this practical joke has been very practical but neglected the joke. I'm not hanging around for the punch line.

She exits.

MOON: Where's she going?

DICKENS: She's not hanging around.

MOON: But she can't get out that way.

MERRIDEW: She and I came in that way.

DEVLIN: You can get almost anywhere from anywhere in these old places if you know your way around. You can also end up going round in circles. If she gets lost, she'll be back.

LARDING: No Château Margaux… *Au revoir mes amis.*

MOON: I'll come with you Oliver. If Al did arrange this I need to have a serious talk with him.

MOON and LARDING exit through the auditorium.

DICKENS: Stage door must be this way somewhere.

He exits upstage.

MERRIDEW: How disappointing. The coquettish promise of an open carriage door has fizzled out completely. Come along girls, let us melt into the metropolitan night and see if we cannot revive the evening.

He exits the same way as PATTERSON.

DEVLIN: I'm still pretty sure it's not a Matcham, but I like it. I'm going to have a look around. George?

MAXWELL: No thanks old boy. I might give 'our host' a little longer to show his blessed face. Give him a piece of my mind. No one does this to George Maxwell.

DEVLIN exits through the opposite wing to PATTERSON and MERRIDEW.

Scene 2

MAXWELL is left alone on stage.

Silence.

He takes a look around him for the first time.

Silence.

He thinks he hears something move.

He thinks he sees something move.

From out of the shadows, something does move.

Some things move, take shape and form into shabby, filthy figures.

They are tramps. Not the homeless of today, but traditional meths-drinking, coat-tied-up-with-string, manky-hat-wearing, straggly-bearded 1970s tramps.

There are six of them. Making themselves comfortable. Drinking their meths.

MAXWELL: What the devil…! You get bloody everywhere don't you. You listen to me. I know what's going on here. I want you off the premises immediately. I will not have this beautiful old theatre turned into a doss house.

The booze-addled tramps ignore him. He starts to prod them with his umbrella.

Come along! Out onto the street with you! This is private property!

He forces the tramps onto their feet with his umbrella, but they do not leave.

Very well. I am going straight to the police who will I am sure throw you into the cells for your trouble. Much to your delight no doubt.

MAXWELL goes as if to leave. The tramps don't exactly prevent him from doing so but some of them seem to gather between him and his exit route and he is driven back by their stinking breath. MAXWELL tries again in a different direction. The same thing happens so he uses his brolly a little more aggressively to try and move them aside. On one occasion his route is blocked when a theatre backdrop depicting ancient Rome descends from the flies.

Come along! Out of my way! You heard me! Out of the way!

The tramps begin to close in on him. They start to push him. Maybe slap him a bit.

Now look here. I won't stand for this.

We'll have no trouble here.

Two uniformed policemen appear. A sergeant and a constable.

Thank goodness.

Although it is clear that MAXWELL is in some difficulty, the policemen do nothing.

These people are trespassing. Would you kindly escort them from the premises.

One of the tramps cuts MAXWELL's arm with a knife. The policemen don't move.

Sergeant!

A little help here.

Another of the tramps cuts MAXWELL's hand. All the tramps produce knives.

Constable! I order you to arrest these people.

The tramps attack, repeatedly stabbing MAXWELL. Finally a slash across the throat causes a huge arc of blood to spatter onto the Roman backdrop.

MAXWELL sinks to the floor. The policemen move over to him.

Why didn't you…?

LIONHEART: O mighty Caesar! Dost thou lie so low?
Are all thy conquests, glories, triumphs, spoils
Shrunk to this little measure?

MAXWELL: You?…I thought you were dead.

LIONHEART: Another critical miscalculation on your part my dear fellow. I am very much alive. It is you who are dead.

MAXWELL dies.

The Sergeant removes his police cape and helmet to reveal the costume of Mark Antony.

The Constable removes his police uniform to reveal a young man dressed as an early seventies COOL DUDE.

The backdrop which has been spattered with blood is torn down and MAXWELL is wrapped in it.

LIONHEART: O! pardon me, thou bleeding piece of earth,
That I am meek and gentle with these butchers;
Over thy wounds now do I prophesy,
Which like dumb mouths do ope their ruby lips,
To beg the voice and utterance of my tongue,
A curse shall light upon the limbs of men;
Blood and destruction shall be so in use,
And dreadful objects so familiar
That my great spirit, ranging for revenge,
With Ate by my side come hot from hell,
Shall in these confines with a monarch's voice
Cry 'Havoc!' and let slip the dogs of war;

The tramps cheer.

COOL DUDE: Let us hear what Antony can say.

LIONHEART: You gentle Romans –

The tramps cheer again.

COOL DUDE: Peace, ho! let us hear him.

LIONHEART: Friends, Romans, countrymen, lend me
                                        your ears;
I come to bury Cæsar, not to praise him.

MAXWELL's body is dragged off stage.

Scene 3

The tramps begin to move scenery around the stage creating a series of very brief scenes that show the critics, in different parts of the building, unable to find a way out.

MERRIDEW appears still holding Cecily and Gwendolen.

MERRIDEW: (*Calling out.*) Sally?… Oh I do wish I'd paid more attention on the way in. (*To his dogs.*) And you're no help. I'm trading you both in for a bloodhound. (*He kisses the dogs affectionately.*)

He exits.

PATTERSON appears. Looks around her as if she heard something. Decides she didn't and exits.

LARDING and MOON appear together.

MOON: Oh do stop chortling Oliver. You sound like a gargling duck. It is very unattractive.

LARDING: I am perfectly happy to admit that I have no idea how to get out of here…

MOON: It's infuriating! I keep thinking I recognise where we came in then it sort of melts away. Why aren't there any bloody exit signs!?

LARDING continues to be amused by her bad temper as they leave.

DICKENS is revealed rattling a door that is clearly locked and then disappears from our view.

The tramps finish the sequence by creating a small room.

The walls are completely covered with newspaper cuttings.

There is also a lectern with a large scrapbook on it.

There are costumes on a rail, among them a costume for Achilles from Troilus *and* Cressida.

Scene 4

PATTERSON enters the room. She looks around for a bit.

The door opens and LIONHEART enters.

LIONHEART: I'll take that winter from your lips, fair lady. Achilles bids you welcome.

My dear Miss Patterson, how pleased I am that you saw fit to investigate the somewhat enigmatic note I sent you.

PATTERSON: Mr Lionheart. You *are* alive. You…are alive. How extraordinary.

LIONHEART: No ordinary tale that no ordinary theatre journalist can tell. Betrayal, suicide, murder…almost as if my very life had taken on a Shakespearean aspect. Of course it is probably of no interest to you. I am but a painted rogue. A dull and muddy mettled rascal.

PATTERSON: It is of great interest…human interest… your survival…your resurrection almost.

LIONHEART: 'Resurrection.' The very word. I always sensed in you Miss Patterson, may I call you Sally? a desire to be more than a mere reviewer. Unlike your colleagues, you yearn for something more real.

PATTERSON: Absolutely. They are stuck in a time warp. I truly believe that unless theatre criticism can change – adapt – it will become extinct.

LIONHEART: It seems we have a sort of understanding.

PATTERSON: I think we do.

LIONHEARAT begins to don the Achilles costume.

LIONHEART: And yet alas t'was not always thus.

PATTERSON: I'm not sure I…

LIONHEART: You have not always 'understood' my work.

PATTERSON: Critics make errors.

LIONHEART: Indeed.

PATTERSON: After all we're only human.

LIONHEART: An opinion I find myself struggling to share.

PATTERSON: You must admit I was most enthusiastic about your performance of Achilles.

LIONHEART: I vaguely remember you wrote a notice of some sort.

PATTERSON: I think I described the production as 'a brilliant theatrical achievement' and I singled out your Achilles as 'unsurpassed'…something like that.

LIONHEART: Splendid. What else did you say?

PATTERSON: Oh, it was all in much the same vein.

LIONHEART: Let me refresh your memory.

LIONHEART refers to the scrapbook. Clearly it contains his press cuttings.

'Edward Lionheart's *Troilus and Cressida* is a brilliant theatrical achievement, and his performance as Achilles – unsurpassed. This is clearly Lionheart's own view. But does he realise how utterly alone he is in his deluded opinion of this lamentable production? No. That is what makes him so ridiculous. He thinks he is incomparable but he is in fact incompetent.'

PATTERSON: Did I write that?

LIONHEART: Your name is Sally Patterson is it not?

PATTERSON: I'm sure you understand it was in no way a personal criticism…

LIONHEART: And then there is the little matter of the Critics' Circle Award for Shakespeare.

PATTERSON: That wasn't my fault.

LIONHEART: You were a member of the committee I understand.

PATTERSON: Yes, but what influence could I have against that cabal of macho dinosaurs? You know what they're like.

LIONHEART: Alas! The complexities of gender politics
are beyond the grasp of a muddle-headed troubadour
such as I, a mere conduit for the great poet. In this case
as in all others my aim was simple. Simply to be
Achilles.

Perhaps if I had my chance again you might feel the full
force of my interpretation?

PATTERSON: I always think theatre is very much a thing
of the moment, once the moment has gone…

*LIONHEART has completed his transformation into Achilles
and he suddenly bursts into full scale acting.*

LIONHEART: Where is this Hector?
Come come thou boy quellor show thy face.
Know what it is to meet Achilles angry.
Hector. Where's Hector? I will none but Hector.

*PATTERSON is suffering that particular squirm making
experience of seeing large acting in a small room.*

PATTERSON: Honestly Mr Lionheart, I would never
question your…commitment to a role.

*The tramps, dressed in rough, thrown-together approximations
of ancient Greek warrior costumes, fill the room. They each
carry a spear.*

LIONHEART: Come here about me, you my Myrmidons;
Mark what I say. Attend me where I wheel:
Strike not a stroke, but keep yourselves in breath:
And when I have the bloody Hector found,
Empale him with your weapons round about;

*LIONHEART and the tramps make as if they are searching
for Hector.*

Follow me, sirs, and my proceedings eye:
It is decreed, Hector the great must die.

Look, Hector, how the sun begins to set;
How ugly night comes breathing at his heels:
Even with the vail and darking of the sun,
To close the day up, Hector's life is done.

PATTERSON: Really Mr Lionheart, what can I say. I am
utterly convinced. This really has been quite an
experience. Theatre on a totally different level.

LIONHEART points at PATTERSON as if she is Hector.

LIONHEART: Strike, fellows, strike! this is the man I seek.

*The tramps turn their spears on PATTERSON. She tries to
get out but can only crawl under the cloth which forms the
back wall of the room.*

*The tramps run around the sides of the cloth. In shadow we
see them run their spears through her body.*

*The back cloth rises to reveal PATTERSON with spears thrust
through her from every angle. She has been lifted off the floor
as if suspended by the radiating poles of a macabre teepee.*

So, Ilion, fall thou next! now, Troy, sink down!
Here lies thy heart, thy sinews, and thy bone.
On! Myrmidons, and cry you all amain,
'Achilles hath the mighty Hector slain.'

A voice calls from offstage.

DEVLIN: Is that you Sally? Are you all right?

LIONHEART: Hark! a retreat upon our Grecian part.

LIONHEART and the tramps exit.

DEVLIN enters, discovers the body and exits.

A set of old red velvet tabs descend to fill the proscenium.

Scene 5

In front of the tabs, LARDING and MOON enter.

LARDING: Honestly Chloë, calm down. This isn't like you. You're not the intuitive type.

MOON: I know, that's what worries me.

LARDING: The intuition? Or that you're not the intuitive type and you're having an intuition?

MOON: Both.

LARDING: Oh Lord.

MERRIDEW enters from the opposite wing with his dogs.

MERRIDEW: Thank goodness! You're still here! Cecily and Gwendolen thought we'd been abandoned.

MOON: We're not 'still here'.

MERRIDEW: My mistake, I thought you were.

MOON: We can't find our way out.

MERRIDEW: Neither can I. Every door I think I came through leads to another door I'm sure I didn't. Every corridor looks the same but none of them look familiar. It's spooky!

MOON: You see! Something is definitely…not right.

LARDING: We can't find our way out of a rambling old building that none of us have been in before. That's all.

MERRIDEW: Gwendolen seems unperturbed, and she is very sensitive to unnatural vibrations.

LARDING: All the others must have found an exit. If they did, we will.

DEVLIN enters.

DEVLIN: We have to get the police! (*Realising they shouldn't be here.*) Why are you still here?

MERRIDEW: The answer to the latter precludes us helping you accomplish the former. Chloë thinks its creepy, Oliver thinks we're dim – why do we need to get the police?

DEVLIN: Sally's dead. Murdered.

Silence.

Sally Patterson. She's dead. I found her downstairs somewhere. She'd been…she's been…she has several, spears…lances…through her…she's standing up.

MERRIDEW: My dear boy, I'm enthralled to find out why you've been hiding such acting talent. I found myself quite chilled.

LARDING: So did I. 'It conveyed a sense of profound shock with an economy rarely seen in the theatre.'

DEVLIN: Sally's dead. We have to get the police. I touched her neck to see…

MOON: You're not joking are you?

DEVLIN: No. I'm not.

LARDING: I'm going to have a look.

MOON: No! We should stay together.

DEVLIN: She's right we should stay together.

LARDING: I don't see why…?

DEVLIN: Because whoever did it might still be here.

MOON: Could we leave now please?

LARDING: We can try.

MOON: Shut up Oliver!

DEVLIN: (*Not sure why MOON is so upset at what LARDING said.*) What?

MERRIDEW: Have you tried getting out of this place?

DEVLIN: No. I was taking a look around. I heard something…

MOON: None of us can find a way out.

MERRIDEW: We keep getting lost and ending up back here.

DEVLIN: Well I first came in through there. Trevor left that way and he's not here so…

MERRIDEW: What about George?

DEVLIN: George I left standing right there.

There is the sound of stage machinery. Sitting in a chair, MAXWELL's blood-spattered body rises up onto the stage through a trap door. A pen and notebook have been placed in his hands.

LARDING: Oh Jesus…

MERRIDEW: I think Gwendolen is going to feint.

DEVLIN approaches the body. He touches it on the neck as if feeling for a pulse.

DEVLIN: He's dead – and cold. Sally was warm. George was killed first.

LARDING: So far so Agatha Christie. According to the rules of the genre the killer must be one of us, or more likely Sally Patterson. Are you sure she was dead?

DEVLIN: I'm sure.

MERRIDEW: I agree. If the murderer turned out to be a character we hadn't met, that would make for a very unsatisfying dénouement.

MOON: How can you talk about genre and dénouement? George has been murdered.

MERRIDEW: Habit I s'pose. After all these years watching…

LARDING: One does tend to look at life through narrative structure.

DEVLIN: And death?

A brief pause. MOON reacts as if she has heard a noise.

MOON: What was that?

MERRIDEW: What?

MOON: I heard something. Someone.

The sound of footsteps approaching.

LARDING: It could be Trevor.

MOON: Sounds like high heels.

MERRIDEW: Each to his own.

MOON: Shhh!

The tabs go out to reveal a rather pretty young woman. She is wearing a summer dress with a floral pattern. She is holding a letter just like the critics received. This is MIRANDA LIONHEART.

MIRANDA: What the hell are you all doing here?

MERRIDEW: We might ask you the same thing. Miss…?

DEVLIN: Lionheart.

LARDING: Yes of course. Edward Lionheart's daughter.

MERRIDEW: Oh God! That appalling actor?

DEVLIN: Hello Miranda.

MIRANDA: I receive a letter asking me to collect some of my father's old costumes and instead I find his murderers.

DEVLIN: We didn't kill your father.

MIRANDA: Perhaps I'm wrong? It was your reverence and understanding that drove him to take his own life? The finest actor of his generation never received one kind or generous word from any of you. Ever. You killed him. You know you killed him.

She notices MAXWELL's body.

What happened?

Looking at them suspiciously.

What happened?

DEVLIN: We found him like that. Sally Patterson is…the same. Somewhere downstairs.

MIRANDA: It was only a matter of time I suppose before someone decided to fight back.

LARDING: Meaning?

MIRANDA: An actor, director, even a producer perhaps, who could find no other way to stop you pouring your poison into the public's ear.

MERRIDEW: Are they going to start killing us for writing bad notices?

MIRANDA: Why not? Careers ended, reputations ruined; lives made unbearable through constant ridicule. That's what killed my father. Plenty of motivation there I should think.

MOON: Can we please get out of here and fetch the police.

DEVLIN: Yes, come along Miranda. We need to report all this.

MIRANDA: I'm not coming with you.

DEVLIN: Don't be stupid.

MIRANDA: I find you with a dead body, (*To DEVLIN.*) your hands smeared with blood and you want me to go with you. Now that would be stupid.

He makes a move towards her and she turns and runs off stage.

DEVLIN: Miranda!

MOON: I am ready to make a sound, the like of which you have never heard unless we get the hell out of here now!

MOON, MERRIDEW and LARDING start to leave.

DEVLIN: We can't leave her here.

MERRIDEW: I'll think you'll find we can dear boy.

DEVLIN: There's a murderous maniac loose in the building.

LARDING: The murderous maniac, in case you hadn't noticed is wearing the hanging gardens of Babylon and she ran thataway.

MOON, MERRIDEW and LARDING exit. DEVLIN runs off after MIRANDA.

Scene 6

LIONHEART and the tramps enter.

The tramps are making the sound of a violent storm with a selection of traditional theatrical devices.

LIONHEART: I will have such revenges on you all
That all the world shall – I will do such things –
What they are yet I know not – but they shall be
The terrors of the earth. You think I'll weep;
No, I'll not weep:
I have full cause of weeping, but this heart
Shall break into a hundred thousand flaws
Or ere I'll weep.

The storm subsides.

My fellows! that art most rich in being poor,
Most choice forsaken and most loved despised,
Thee and thy virtues here I seize upon.
Be it lawful I take up what's cast away.

I little thought that when we chanced upon
Each other, fortune would provide for me
So worthy a supporting company.
These deeds of quaint brutality you have
Fulfilled with sturdy hands and yet I feel
A spark of something more than this which stirs
Within your souls.

Your range will remain firmly of the mechanicals, the
rustics and the simpletons but even they, with His words
may speak truth…

…and perhaps there are some among you that might
speak more than truth…

Lift up thy looks.

LIONHEART notices one of the female tramps.

Thou dearest Perdita,

This is the prettiest low-born lass that ever
Ran on the greensward: nothing she does or seems
But smacks of something greater than herself;
Too noble for this place.

Come, quench your blushes and present yourself
That which you are, Mistress o'th'Feast

*The other tramps begin to remove her tatty clothes, brush out
her hair, clean her face and dress her in beautiful fashionable
clothes. The atmosphere is very tender and magical. A
transformation of her sense of self, as well as of her
appearance.*

LIONHEART sings.

Lawn as white as driven snow;
Cyprus black as e'er was crow;
Gloves as sweet as damask roses;
Masks for faces and for noses;
Bugle-bracelet, necklace-amber,
Perfume for a lady's chamber;
Golden quoifs and stomachers,
For my lads to give their dears;
Pins and poking-sticks of steel;
What maids lack from head to heel:
Come buy of me, come; come buy, come buy;
Buy, lads, or else your lasses cry:
Come buy.

Will you buy any tape,
Or lace for your cape,
My dainty duck, my dear-a?
Any silk, any thread,
Any toys for your head,
Of the new'st and fin'st, fin'st wear-a?
Come to the pedlar;
Money's a meddler,
That doth utter all men's ware-a.

The transformation is complete.

Sure this robe of thine
Does change thy disposition.

My prettiest…! A princess – she
The fairest I have yet beheld
                                    Be merry, gentle;
Address yourself to entertain him sprightly,

PERDITA: I will enchant the old and lech'rous man
With words more sweet, and yet more dangerous,
Than baits to fish, or honey-stalks to sheep,
When as the one is wounded with the bait,
The other rotted with delicious feed.

LIONHEART and the tramps exit, leaving the girl alone.

Scene 7

TREVOR DICKENS enters. He sees the young woman.

DICKENS: Hello there.

PERDITA: Mr Dickens! You've found me. I'm so pleased
you came.

DICKENS: It's all been a little confusing to be honest. You
must be…

PERDITA: Perdita Stevens. When I wrote the letter I never
thought for a moment that you would agree to help us,
you're such an important man.

DICKENS: It is our duty to nurture young talent. I – no
hang on a minute, why did you ask the others to…?

PERDITA: That was rather naughty of us. We are a young
company so to get some attention from the press we
played a trick on them. Only you came here for
unselfish reasons and you are the only one we hope can
offer us a guiding hand.

DICKENS: Oh, I see…

*DICKENS seems a little confused, but he is not confused
about how attractive he finds this young woman.*

PERDITA: We are developing a new form that we call 'Living Theatre'. It requires a man of vision to guide it at this early stage. From your writing I feel you are just such a man, and meeting you in the flesh makes me think so even more. I want to experience everything, and there are some things that only a man of your experience can show me.

DICKENS: I'll certainly endeavour to...er...to...erm...er... tell me a little more about this 'Living Theatre'.

PERDITA: To get people really involved in the performance, a member of the audience comes up on stage to play the protagonist.

DICKENS: I see. And you'd like me to watch a rehearsal.

PERDITA: Oh no! I want you to be in the rehearsal. I want you to feel it from the inside.

DICKENS: Well I'm...

PERDITA: It is a private rehearsal. I'll be with you the whole time to make sure you have everything you need. I'd be so grateful...

DICKENS: If you really feel I have something to offer...

PERDITA: Oh thank you!

She kisses him. As she does the tramps reappear to set up the courtroom scene from The Merchant of Venice. *There is a witness box, in which DICKENS stands, and a set of scales.*

LIONHEART appears as Shylock in the full get-up; putty nose and everything. COOL DUDE is Portia as the Lawyer.

COOL DUDE: Antonio and old Shylock, both stand forth.

DICKENS: *Merchant of Venice* eh!... Hmm, tricky one to carry off.

COOL DUDE: Is your name Shylock?

LIONHEART: Shylock is my name.

COOL DUDE: You stand within his danger, do you not?

PERDITA: You're playing Antonio.

DICKENS gets a script.

In our version, Antonio is a promiscuous womaniser. I play his latest conquest.

DICKENS: I suppose that is a way of eliciting some sympathy for Shylock. How clever… I'm not sure it is supported by the text…

COOL DUDE: You stand within his danger, do you not?

PERDITA points to the line on his script that DICKENS has to say.

DICKENS: (*Rather quietly.*) Ay, so he says.

PERDITA signals for him to speak the line again but louder – with more feeling.

Ay, so he says.

COOL DUDE: Do you confess the bond?

DICKENS: (*Starting to enjoy himself.*) I do.

COOL DUDE: Then must the Jew be merciful.

LIONHEART: On what compulsion must I? tell me that.

COOL DUDE: The quality of mercy is not strain'd,
It droppeth as the gentle rain from heaven
Upon the place beneath: it is twice bless'd;
It blesseth him that gives and him that takes:
'Tis mightiest in the mighty; it becomes
The throned monarch better than his crown;
But mercy is above this sceptred sway,

It is enthroned in the hearts of kings,
It is an attribute to God himself,
And earthly power doth then show likest God's
When mercy seasons justice.

LIONHEART: My deeds upon my head! I crave the law,
The penalty and forfeit of my bond.

COOL DUDE: I pray you, let me look upon the bond.

LIONHEART: Here 'tis, most reverend doctor; here it is.

COOL DUDE: Why, this bond is forfeit;
And lawfully by this the Jew may claim
A pound of flesh, to be by him cut off
Nearest the merchant's heart.

DICKENS is really in the swing of it now – wishing he had more lines.

DICKENS: Most heartily I do beseech the court
To give the judgment.

COOL DUDE: Why then, thus it is:
You must prepare your bosom for his knife.

DICKENS is laid on a table. A set of brutal looking surgical instruments is offered to LIONHEART on a tray.

LIONHEART: O noble judge! O excellent young man!

COOL DUDE: Therefore lay bare your bosom.

LIONHEART: 'Nearest his heart': those are the very words.

COOL DUDE: You, merchant, have you anything to say?

DICKENS: But little: I am arm'd and well prepar'd.

COOL DUDE: A pound of that same merchant's flesh is
thine:
The court awards it, and the law doth give it.

LIONHEART: Most rightful judge!

COOL DUDE: And you must cut this flesh from off his breast:
　　The law allows it, and the court awards it.

LIONHEART: Most learned judge! A sentence! come,
　　　　　　　　　　　　　　　　　　prepare!

LIONHEART has the knife poised above DICKENS' chest.
DICKENS is acting being scared.

COOL DUDE: Tarry a little: there is something else.
　　This bond doth give thee here no jot of blood;
　　The words expressly are 'a pound of flesh':
　　But, in the cutting it, if thou dost shed
　　One drop of Christian blood, thy lands and goods
　　Are, by the laws of Venice, confiscate
　　Unto the state of Venice.

LIONHEART: Is that the law?

COOL DUDE: Thyself shalt see the act;

LIONHEART: Then confiscate my lands and goods for by
　　Our holy Sabbath have I sworn that I
　　Will have the due and forfeit of my bond.

LIONHEART plunges the knife into DICKENS' chest.
DICKENS reaches out and grabs LIONHEART's putty nose
which comes off in his hand.

DICKENS: Lionheart!

LIONHEART: My Shylock was an ignoble insult to the
　　Jewish nation was he?

DICKENS: No! No!

LIONHEART has pushed his hand inside DICKENS' body
and is rooting around, trying to get at his heart.

LIONHEART: My Shylock is noble enough not to bow to
Portia's piece of pettifogging legal trickery. Perhaps you
can see that now?

DICKENS: You were the best! I always said you were the
best!

LIONHEART: Ah! – the best is given the Critics' Circle
Award.

DICKENS: It was Devlin…Devlin!

LIONHEART: Hand me that crowbar, I need to snap a
couple of ribs if I am to get to his shrivelled little heart.

*The crowbar is handed to LIONHEART and he goes to work
on DICKENS' ribcage.*

DICKENS: Why?… Why?

LIONHEART: Why?

You have disgraced me, and hindered me, laughed at my
losses, mocked my gains, cooled my friends, heated mine
enemies; and what's the reason? I am an actor. Hath not
an actor eyes? hath not an actor hands, organs,
dimensions, senses, affections, passions? If you prick us,
do we not bleed? if you tickle us, do we not laugh? if
you poison us, do we not die? and if you wrong us, shall
we not revenge?

*We hear a final crack as DICKENS' ribs come away.
LIONHEART digs around for a moment then emerges with
the heart. He and Portia take it to the scales and weigh it.*

LIONHEART: It was a pound exactly was it not?

COOL DUDE: A pound the bond doth say, no more no less.

LIONHEART: This is two ounces over

He cuts a little off.

There! 'Tis done.

COOL DUDE: Art thou content?

LIONHEART: I am content.

All exit, leaving only the heart and the scales.

Scene 8

DEVLIN enters. He sees the heart in the scales.

MIRANDA enters. She sees the heart in the scales.

MIRANDA: Is that what I think it is?

DEVLIN: I think it is.

MIRANDA: Whose?

DEVLIN: No idea, but it looks fresh.

MIRANDA: You're a dangerous man to be around.

DEVLIN: Your father's body was never found was it?

MIRANDA: My father is dead. You saw him die. You and your pack needn't fear he's come back to haunt you.

DEVLIN: But his body was never found.

MIRANDA: He's dead, let him be. You can't hurt him any more. That's why he threw himself off that building. So none of you could hurt him any more.

DEVLIN: Who else would do this?

MIRANDA: He isn't the only one. Every day you decide whose work will live and whose work will die. I'm only surprised that it hasn't happened before. Yours is a dangerous job Mr Devlin. Someone should have told you that.

Why were you so vicious to my father? He devoted his life to acting. He believed – rightly or wrongly – that theatre could change people into something more than themselves. All he ever got from you was ridicule and spite.

DEVLIN: A critic begins to resent an actor he has to keep giving bad reviews. I'm sorry. No one doubted his passion, but he…he made himself ridiculous. How many years had it been since he'd appeared in a leading role at a London theatre? How many years since he'd played anything anywhere? Suddenly there was an entire season of Shakespeare produced by and starring him. And from the first performance it was clear he thought nothing had changed in the last twenty or thirty years. He never stood a chance.

MIRANDA: You never gave him a chance.

DEVLIN: It was embarrassing. He was frozen in time but not that well preserved. Immovable in his own belief of what Shakespeare should be.

MIRANDA: A heretic to be burned?

DEVLIN: Just not good enough. He couldn't wake up. Play after play through the season; exactly the same way. Whatever we said, he didn't seem to hear it.

MIRANDA: He heard it.

DEVLIN: Perhaps I should have lied! Said I found his productions relevant, thrilling, revelatory. I didn't realise my job was to stroke the ego of every puffed up peacock that climbs into a doublet and hose under the misapprehension that only they understand Shakespeare! I was just being honest.

MIRANDA: Maybe so. But when you were writing those witty, sarcastic lines can you honestly tell me that you didn't enjoy it?

He shows her a poster.

DEVLIN: I found this. It's for that season of Shakespeare. Notice anything?

MIRANDA: I know that he sold his house and everything he owned: his most precious possessions. Everything. His whole life was staked on that season.

DEVLIN: First play *Julius Caesar*. Caesar is stabbed to death by several assassins on the Ides of March, the 15th – today. You saw George Maxwell. Next, *Troilus and Cressida* in which Hector is surrounded by Achilles' Myrmidons and 'empaled' with 'weapons round about'. Sally Patterson was… Third in the season is *The Merchant of Venice*. In this version, Shylock took his pound of flesh. Only Lionheart would have the temerity to re-write Shakespeare.

MIRANDA: The ghost of my father takes revenge on his critics by arranging Shakespearean deaths for them all? How exactly do I fit into this fantastical theory of yours? Be realistic.

DEVLIN: I'm in a theatre no one can leave. Every time I turn around I see another mutilated corpse. The only thing that makes any sense is this (*Indicating the poster.*) …I stepped out of reality when I walked into this theatre.

MIRANDA: Isn't that supposed to happen when you walk into a theatre? The most obvious suspect is me. I have more reason to hate you all than anyone alive. Do you think I'm doing all this?

DEVLIN: No.

MIRANDA: I can't believe he's alive. I won't let myself believe he's alive. It's taken me too long to accept that he's dead.

DEVLIN: If you're here, you're in danger. We all are. That much we do know.

A voice from offstage.

LIONHEART: Fetch me my rapier, boy. What, dares the slave
Come hither, covered with an antic face,
To fleer and scorn at our solemnity?

DEVLIN: Is that your father?

MIRANDA: I don't know. I don't know if I want it to be
him. Not if he's become... I don't know.

DEVLIN: You'd better get out of here.

MIRANDA: What about you?

DEVLIN: I'd rather meet him face to face than run around
waiting to be skewered.

While he's here, you're safe to try and find a way out and
get help.

From offstage:

LIONHEART: Now, by the stock and honour of my kin,
To strike him dead I hold it not a sin.

DEVLIN: Go on!

MIRANDA exits.

Scene 9

DEVLIN: Here I am then! What are you waiting for?

A sword is thrown onto the stage.

I said what are you waiting for?

LIONHEART enters. He is holding a sword.

LIONHEART: Boy, I shall not excuse the injuries
That thou hast done me. Therefore turn and draw.

DEVLIN: Lionheart!

DEVLIN picks up the sword.

LIONHEART: Alive in triumph! And you thought me slain.

The duel begins. They occasionally pause to deliver their verbal thrusts.

Your reputation as a rising star of the Putney and Roehampton Fencing Club is well deserved.

DEVLIN: Perhaps you'll regret handing me this rapier?

LIONHEART: I think not Devlin thy head stands so tickle on thy shoulders, that a milkmaid, if she be in love, may sigh it off.

DEVLIN: If anyone's about to lose their head…

LIONHEART: Ha! Lionheart is immortal. He can never be destroyed. Never…Never…!

What's the matter Devlin? Did you not say of my Mercutio that 'he handled his sword as if he were attempting to spear the last pickled onion in the jar'? It seems you are learning that make believe is more real than you thought.

LIONHEART swipes at a rope and a sandbag falls from the flies and nearly hits DEVLIN.

They fight again and DEVLIN disarms LIONHEART.

DEVLIN: Why, Lionheart?

LIONHEART: You know why dear boy. You above them all know why.

DEVLIN: Oh dear. The same mistake that so many actors make: Critics? You take them too seriously. They're just reviews.

LIONHEART: He jests at scars that never felt a wound.

DEVLIN: Oh come on Lionheart! What 'wound'?

LIONHEART has backed up against one of the wings. He reaches behind him and produces an enormous broadsword.

LIONHEART: Death for death!
Haste still pays haste, and leisure answers leisure;
Like doth quit like, and Measure still for Measure.

LIONHEART disarms DEVLIN and has him at his mercy.

DEVLIN: Death for death? You must be running low on
quotations Lionheart. Sally never killed anyone. George
never killed anyone.

LIONHEART: How many actors have you destroyed, as
you destroyed me? How many talented lives have you
cut down with your glib attacks?

No, Devlin, no.
I am a man more sinned against than sinning.

I did not murder George Maxwell and the others.
Punished them my dear boy, punished them. Just as you
shall have to be punished.

DEVLIN: Get it over with then. I'd rather die than listen to
that demented rubbish of yours. You don't care anything
for the 'noble profession' you're just ticked off because
we gave the Critics' Circle Award for Shakespeare to
William Woodstock.

LIONHEART: Ye gods, it doth amaze me,
A man of such a feeble temper should
So get the start of the majestic world,
And bear the palm alone.

DEVLIN: So much for thespian solidarity.

Several tramps appear and grab hold of DEVLIN.

Who the hell are this lot?

LIONHEART: My fellows. My colleagues. My company.

DEVLIN: How did you survive Lionheart. Why aren't you dead?

LIONHEART: My dear Devlin. You find yourself overpowered and you ask me to move into exposition. A piece of plotting that surely would have earned your withering sarcasm should you have seen it from the stalls.

It's not so easy when you're in it – is it?

Still, who am I to deny the request of such an eminent audience and the scene does finale with a fine soliloquy from yours truly.

Scene 10

LIONHEART: The time: a year ago today. The place: your sumptuous penthouse apartment boasting fine views of the river. The cast: you and your artistically myopic cronies who had adjourned for a post-award ceremony drink.

A truck appears at the back of the stage and travels down. On the truck is a trendy seventies flat. The back wall is glass with a door leading out onto a balcony. In the distance we can see a view of the Thames and the new National Theatre building.

All the critics are there, drinking and chatting. One of the tramps is playing DEVLIN. They are dressed in evening wear. Prominent is a statuette of Shakespeare: The Critics' Circle Award.

DEVLIN recognises his own flat.

DEVLIN: But that's my… (*Calling out to the apparently unharmed critics.*) George! George!! Sally!

LIONHEART: Shout all you like my dear Devlin. They cannot hear you.

These are spirits
Which by mine art I have from their confines
Called to enact my present fancies.
Hush and be mute, or else our spell is marred.

What do you think of the casting? Probably they all look exactly right except you. It's like that for everyone. Like hearing your voice on a tape recorder; it's never quite as you think it is. You must excuse me. I'm on in a moment.

LIONHEART exits.

DEVLIN 2 picks up the award.

DEVLIN 2: It's a shame William is on tour and wasn't there to pick this up.

MERRIDEW: I think Lionheart was ready to do the honours.

LARDING: I know. Actually got to his feet just as you were giving us your 'And the award goes to…'!

MOON: When you said 'William Woodstock', he just stood there…

PATTERSON: Oh God! I nearly died!

MAXWELL: Hadn't the faintest idea what was going on.

DICKENS: Poor fella. Deluded.

DEVLIN 2: Apart from that minor hiccup, I thought it went very well. (*He raises his glass. The other critics do likewise.*) To William Woodstock – a worthy winner.

DEVLIN 2 notices that the other critics have stopped listening to him and are looking past him to the door. He turns to see LIONHEART standing there.

Lionheart – what the hell do you want here?

LIONHEART stands silently for a moment in the doorway. Then walks calmly over and takes hold of the award.

LIONHEART: This. My just reward. The whole world knows it is mine by right. You have deliberately withheld it from me, deliberately humiliated me before the press, my public and my peers. It was the culmination of your persistent denial of my genius.

DEVLIN 2: We've denied you nothing.

LIONHEART: The public and the profession acknowledge that I am the Master – and that this year my season of Shakespeare was the shining jewel in the crown of the immortal bard.

DICKENS: Quite insane.

LARDING: Must be drunk.

LIONHEART: And you – with your over-weaning malice give the award to a twitching mumbling boy, who can barely grunt his way through an incomprehensible performance. No! No! It is mine!

MIRANDA, also in an evening dress, enters.

MIRANDA: Father…

DEVLIN: (*Calling out to her.*) Miranda?

She doesn't respond.

MIRANDA: Father, please come away. You mustn't do this. You are only helping them to hurt you more.

They look into each other's eyes, and for a moment it seems to bring him to his senses.

LIONHEART: Miranda… Oh my God – what have I done…?

MIRANDA: Father…?

MERRIDEW: Bless my soul, we've got the entire family.

LIONHEART: To be, or not to be: that is the question:
Whether 'tis nobler in the mind to suffer
The slings and arrows of outrageous fortune,
Or to take arms against a sea of troubles,
And by opposing end them? To die: to sleep;
No more; and, by a sleep to say we end
The heart-ache and the thousand natural shocks
That flesh is heir to, 'tis a consummation
Devoutly to be wish'd. To die, to sleep;
To sleep: perchance to dream: ay, there's the rub;
For in that sleep of death what dreams may come
When we have shuffled off this mortal coil,
Must give us pause.

LIONHEART goes out onto the balcony.

MAXWELL: The fellow's ga-ga.

PATTERSON: Embarrassing.

MOON: Watching him act always is.

MIRANDA: Butchers!

LIONHEART: There's the respect
That makes calamity of so long life.

Still holding the award, LIONHEART jumps off the balcony.

Scene 11

DEVLIN's flat begins to truck upstage and out of sight.

LIONHEART appears in a box on the proscenium impossibly quickly.

LIONHEART: I hope you'll agree that I'm being even
handed with the facts.

DEVLIN: But my flat is on the fourteenth floor…

47

LIONHEART: O I am as the air, invulnerable,

The last you see of me, is as I disappear from your
balcony.

And from that highest promontory top.
Down, down I come, like glist'ring Phaëton.
Accoutrèd as I was, I plungèd in
…thrown in the Thames like a barrow of butcher's offal

*LIONHEART jumps from the proscenium box and flies into
an underwater fantasy. The tramps animate little sea creatures
and some of the things that LIONHEART mentions as
LIONHEART floats/flies around them.*

Lord, Lord! methought what pain it was to drown:
What dreadful noise of water in mine ears!
What sights of ugly death within mine eyes!
Methought I saw a thousand fearful wracks;
A thousand men that fishes gnaw'd upon;
Wedges of gold, great anchors, heaps of pearl,
Inestimable stones, unvalu'd jewels,
All scatter'd in the bottom of the sea.
Some lay in dead men's skulls; and in those holes
Where eyes did once inhabit, there were crept,
As 'twere in scorn of eyes, reflecting gems,
That woo'd the slimy bottom of the deep,
And mock'd the dead bones that lay scatter'd by.

Had I such leisure in the time of death
To gaze upon those secrets of the deep?
Methought I had; and often did I strive
To yield the ghost; but still the envious flood
Stopt in my soul, and would not let it forth.
O Lionheart, be absolute for death;

*An image of MIRANDA appears before LIONHEART. She
is tearing at a small bunch of flowers and herbs. An echo of
Ophelia.*

MIRANDA: And will he not come again?
And will he not come again?
No, no, he is dead;
Go to thy death-bed,
He never will come again.

LIONHEART: Full fathom five thy father lies;
Of his bones are coral made:
Those are pearls that were his eyes:
Nothing of him that doth fade,
But doth suffer a sea-change
Into something rich and strange.
Sea-nymphs hourly ring his knell:
Hark! now I hear them – ding-dong, bell.

...suffer a sea-change

a change...

Into something rich and strange.

MIRANDA exits.

The atmosphere changes and becomes more ominous. Emerging from the murky water are the great actors of history. They are the actors we saw in the Prologue.

Their performances are of course as huge, expansive and magnificent as you (or LIONHEART) would expect such legends to be.

Henry Irving
I shame to hear thee speak. Ah, timorous wretch!
Thou hast undone thyself,

Richard Burbage
To think of what a noble strain you are,
And of how coward a spirit.

Edith Evans
I never saw an action of such shame;
Experience, manhood, honour, ne'er before
Did violate so itself.

Sarah Siddons
Wise men ne'er sit and wail their loss,
But cheerly seek how to redress their harms.

David Garrick
Now, afore God, 'tis shame such wrongs are borne

Beerbohm Tree
Thou great-sized coward…
Hope of revenge should hide thy inward woe.

Sarah Bernhardt
Oft have I heard that grief softens the mind,
And makes it fearful and degenerate;
Think therefore on revenge and cease to weep.

Ellen Terry
Be comforted:
Let's make us medicines of our great revenge,
To cure this deadly grief.

Edmund Kean
Wilt thou revenge?

Ghost Actors
Adieu, adieu, adieu. Remember me.

The great actors of history exit.

LIONHEART: O all you host of heaven! O earth! What else?
And shall I couple hell?

*LIONHEART is cast down onto the floor. He lies completely
still. We can hear the sound of water lapping on a shoreline.
He has been swept onto the bank of the river. Washed up
beside him is the Critics' Circle Award.*

LIONHEART points an accusing finger at DEVLIN.

The pretty vaulting sea refus'd to drown me,
Knowing that thou wouldst have me drown'd on shore
With tears as salt as sea through thy unkindness:

LIONHEART passes out. The tramps enter. They approach him warily. They go through his pockets, examine his clothes and the award which is lying by his side.

Then they pick him up and take him to the theatre. They lay him down and make him comfortable. Then they make themselves comfortable and go to sleep.

Scene 12

LIONHEART begins to stir. He opens his eyes, gradually coming back to his senses. He looks around him.

LIONHEART: O, wonder!
How many goodly creatures are there here!
How beauteous mankind is! O, brave new world,
That has such people in't!
Am I in earth, in heaven, or in hell?

He looks at himself. Sees that he is in a theatre. He comes to a delicate and delicious realisation.

In earth. In heaven, but no more in hell.
Not sleeping but awake and well-advised
Since I am no more to myself disguised!

O what was I? O what had I become?
That craved the love of those that cannot love?
That searched outside myself for what myself
Should be, as if the eye sees not itself
But by reflection, by some other things.

Abhorred treacherous army that i'th dead
Of darkness sit with all my faults observ'd,
Set in a note-book, learn'd, and conn'd by rote,
To cast into my teeth.

O! I could weep.
Me from myself thy cruel words hath taken!
Till I myself was to myself not mine.

Mine eyes are full of tears, I cannot see:
And yet salt water blinds them not so much
But they can see your loathsome treachery.
Nay, if I turn mine eyes upon myself,
I find myself a traitor with the rest;
For I have given here my soul's consent
To undeck the pompous body of a king;
Made glory base and sovereignty a slave,
Proud majesty a subject, state a peasant.
And this hath made me traitor to myself.

O me! the fault it is not in our stars,
But in ourselves, that we are underlings.
I know not why We put a sting in him
That at his will he may do danger with.

No more. My other self is dead, it lies
Inside a muddy ditch, close by the Thames.

Presume not that I am the thing I was;
For God doth know, so shall the world perceive,
That I have turn'd away my former self;

I will from henceforth rather be myself,
Mighty and to be fear'd,

Away with slavish weeds and servile thoughts!
I shall forget myself to be myself.

And yet who am I? What am I?…
Well, I will proclaim myself what I am…

I am very proud, revengeful, ambitious, with more
offences at my beck than I have thoughts to put them in,
imagination to give them shape, or time to act them in.

I am I

I am an actor…

Why, I can smile, and murder whiles I smile,
And cry 'Content' to that which grieves my heart,
And wet my cheeks with artificial tears,

And frame my face to all occasions.
I'll drown more sailors than the mermaid shall;
I'll slay more gazers than the basilisk;
I'll play the orator as well as Nestor,
I can add colours to the chameleon,
Change shapes with Proteus for advantages,
And set the murderous Machiavel to school.
Can I do this and cannot get revenge?

So every actor in his own hand bears
The power to cancel his captivity.

I know myself now; and I feel within me
A peace above all earthly dignities,
Vengeance is in my heart, death in my hand,
Blood and revenge are hammering in my head.
And in the closing of some glorious day
Then I will wear a garment all of blood
And stain my favours in a bloody mask,
Which, wash'd away, shall scour my shame with it:
For mighty God in heaven hath pleased it so,
To punish me with this and this with me,
That I must be their scourge and minister

I'm hungry for revenge. So shall you hear
Of carnal, bloody, and unnatural acts,
Of accidental judgments, casual slaughters,
Of deaths put on by cunning and forc'd cause,
Then kill, kill, kill, kill, kill, kill!

How light and portable my pain seems now,

O! from this time forth,
My thoughts be bloody, or be nothing worth!

The theatre tabs descend, separating DEVLIN from LIONHEART and the tramps.

DEVLIN: Lionheart!

INTERVAL

Scene 13

MOON, MERRIDEW and LARDING are in a dressing room. There is a mirror with lights around it in the traditional manner (not all of them work); a table with some make up on it; a clothes rail with costumes on hangers (the costumes we have seen LIONHEART wearing); and a couple of comfortable looking chairs.

The room employs the theatrical convention whereby there are no walls, but the boundaries of the space are defined by furniture and props which would be placed against the walls.

There is a free standing door in a frame which helps to define the limits of the room. The door is closed.

LARDING is trying to open this door which will not budge. He has been trying for some time.

MOON: How could you let the door close behind us like that?

LARDING: I didn't realise that I'd been delegated responsibility for doors.

MOON: In our present situation it seems obvious that you wouldn't go into a room and let the door shut without making sure that you could open it again.

LARDING: If it's so fucking obvious why didn't you say so as we came in here?

MOON: Because it's fucking obvious!

MERRIDEW: Please! (*Putting his hands over Cecily's ears.*) My babies are not used to such industrial colloquialisms.

LARDING: Well they'd better fucking get used to it fucking quick because things could get a lot more fucking industrial before we get fucking out of fucking here.

And just for good measure:

Fucking.

MERRIDEW: Ooooh Oliver, I imagine that is more fucking than you've done in a long while.

LARDING: When are you going to stop it?

MERRIDEW: Stop what dear boy?

LARDING: This persona, this…act, this cultivated cartoon of perfumed eccentricity. Do you imagine people regard you as a character? That it fulfils our ideal of the waspish wit? The lavender *bon vivant* who takes nothing seriously except the seriously trivial? I mean do you do it when you're alone…just you and your fucking poodles? Or what about when you're fucking one of your rent boys; as he's finishing you off…? as you hand over the money…? do you remain the prancing dandy throughout? What if you're next and the killer finds you alone? When the knife plunges into your plenteous belly and the blood gurgles out of your gasping lips, will you still be wracking your brains for a cheap *bon mot*? A last snide comment? Or might you finally, finally take something seriously?

MERRIDEW: My my Oliver, you *do* need a drink.

LARDING: Yes I need a drink. My God I need a drink!

MOON: I don't suppose anyone would like to think about how we might open this door?

LARDING: It's a dead bolt lock but it's not locked. I don't know why it won't open.

MOON: Break it down then.

MERRIDEW: This is not Hollywood my dear. In the real world doors are made to be stronger than the human frame. That is their *raison d'être*. If we could just break them down willy nilly, there'd be no point in having them.

MOON: Alan would do it.

LARDING: Alan would certainly try.

MOON: Yes! Because he's a man! A real man. Alan would simply run headlong at that door and break it down.

LARDING: And since his biggest organ is not his brain, only when he had shattered most of his bones would he realise that the door opens inwards.

MOON: But if we can't get out…

LARDING: Once we're missed they'll come looking for us.

MOON: Nobody knows we're here.

LARDING: Michael's taxi driver…

MERRIDEW: I'm one of his regulars.

LARDING: There's Trevor – once he gets over not giving a leg up to a keen student actress… George will have told everyone he was coming here to get a job at the National and Peter will fetch the police as soon as he stops chasing Miss Lionheart.

MOON: Do you think she killed George?

MERRIDEW: And Sally.

MOON: I keep forgetting about Sally.

LARDING: After what happened last year at Peter's flat it must be her.

MOON: Yes it must be.

MERRIDEW: I simply cannot see how she can blame us for what happened.

MOON: Unhinged, like her father.

LARDING: (*Indicating the costume rail.*) She did say she was here to pick up her father's costumes.

MERRIDEW: When she found us all together – first thing that came to mind.

LARDING: She attacked George and Sally when they were alone, she couldn't take on a group of us.

The idea that they know who the killer is, and that it is a young girl seems to calm them a little. There is a short silence.

MOON: We're probably safer in here till help arrives.

LARDING: Exactly.

MOON: Poor George.

LARDING: Sweet man.

MERRIDEW: Yes.

Of course he would have been totally wrong for that job at the National.

LARDING: Totally wrong.

MOON: He's the wrong man totally.

LARDING: Although I do think a critical perspective inside the building will be important.

MERRIDEW: Vital.

LARDING: Having a theatre director in overall control makes no sense to me.

MOON: How will they direct their own work alongside other productions and not be accused of bias in the allocation of budgets and so on?

MERRIDEW: The whole place will become the personal fiefdom of an artistic ego.

LARDING: I think there should be an Intendant in overall control.

MOON: Someone with a deep understanding of theatre.

LARDING: But not personally involved in the business of directing plays.

MERRIDEW: I certainly wouldn't want to do it. All those deathly dull committees.

MOON: God! It would be a nightmare!

LARDING: Absolute nightmare. Yes. Absolutely.

MERRIDEW: Of course you know the reason George was so keen to find another post was that I'd been offered his job at the *Telegraph*.

MOON: No!

MERRIDEW: And I think he'd got wind.

LARDING: What?

MERRIDEW: Of the fact that I'd been offered his job.

LARDING: Oh I see.

MOON: Did you take it?

MERRIDEW: Yes, the offer was very good. But then my lot offered me more to stay, so I stayed. But by then George had been somewhat undermined.

The tramps appear in the shadows around the edge of the stage. They have attempted to dress as posh wine buffs. They each hold wine bottles up to their lips and blow across the top to create eerie music.

LARDING: Someone is going to get George's job. And Sally's. It's terrible what has happened…

MERRIDEW: But the reviews must go on.

MOON begins to yawn.

MOON: I can't think why I'm suddenly so tired.

She sits in the reclining chair and yawns again. MERRIDEW yawns and sits in the other chair.

MERRIDEW: Don't. You'll start me off.

LIONHEART's voice seems to drift in from the shadows, as if it is coming from inside MOON and MERRIDEW's heads.

LIONHEART: Thou art inclin'd to sleep; 'tis a good dullness, And give it way; – I know thou canst not choose

MOON and MERRIDEW each make themselves comfortable ready to take a nap.

LARDING: Are you two alright?

Almost asleep now.

MOON: Fine. Just. Heavy.

MERRIDEW begins to snore and then MOON is asleep.

Gwendolen and Cecily jump out of MERRIDEW's arms and run off stage through one of the imaginary walls of the room.

LARDING watches the dogs go and seems to see the set for what it is; a room with no walls.

He gingerly approaches one of the walls and gently steps through it. He smiles to himself at the oddness of what has just happened.

Scene 14

Some of the tramps remove the dressing room, including MERRIDEW and MOON, still asleep in their chairs. Others entrance LARDING with the bottles of wine. Clearly these are fantastic vintages. One of the tramps pours LARDING a glass of something rare and delicious. He sniffs at it, but is too suspicious to take a sip.

COOL DUDE enters.

COOL DUDE: Can I see your invitation sir?

LARDING: I beg your pardon?

COOL DUDE: I need to see your invitation sir or I will have to ask you to unhand that glass of Vieux Château Certan '59.

LARDING: Look the only invitation I received was this letter, and I'd like to know if you know anything about it…

He produces the letter from his pocket and unfolds it but to his surprise, folded inside the letter he finds an embossed card – an invitation to a wine tasting.

COOL DUDE takes the card.

COOL DUDE: Thank you sir. Ah, Mr Larding. We're honoured.

LARDING: Could I see that?

She hands the card back to him.

'Richard Clarence Wine Importation.' Never heard of it.

COOL DUDE: We are a new company, which is why we are holding this tasting, and why you are holding that Certan '59.

LARDING looks at the wine in his hand. He would love to taste it but daren't.

LARDING: Would you like to taste it?

COOL DUDE: That's hardly…

LARDING: I insist.

The COOL DUDE takes the glass and expertly sniffs then sips. He is clearly transported by the delights of the wine.

COOL DUDE: Incredibly complex but utterly direct. Almost overwhelming.

I'll fetch another glass…

LARDING is positively salivating.

LARDING: No, no! This one will be fine.

He takes the glass from COOL DUDE and devours a noseful and then a mouthful of the wine.

It is a better-than-sex experience.

He suddenly pauses as if waiting for some poison to take effect, but nothing happens except the ecstatic glow of fine wine.

LARDING notices another bottle.

An Haut Brion!? It's not…it can't be…

COOL DUDE: The '61.

LARDING: It is!

COOL DUDE: If you would like to come with me to the cellars ladies and gentlemen. We have excellent representation from several rare vintages including a Montrachet '64, a Lafite Rothschild '61 and a Château Margaux '59.

LARDING: Margaux…'59!

LARDING, COOL DUDE and the wine tasters exit.

LIONHEART appears as Richard III.

LIONHEART: I am determined to prove a villain
And hate the idle pleasures of these days.
Plots have I laid, inductions dangerous,
By drunken prophecies, libels and dreams,
That Clarence here should closely be mewed up.

LIONHEART reads from his scrapbook.

Well now Larding…

'Edward Lionheart as Richard III bored the doublet and hose off me, till at last I found merciful relief in the land of nod.'

Well, we shall see if we cannot stir you into more rapt attention with tonight's performance.

COOL DUDE, LARDING and the wine tasters return. The tramps bring with them a large barrel of wine.

Dive, thoughts, down to my soul: here Clarence comes.

COOL DUDE: And now *the* wine of the evening. The Margaux '59. As the foremost expert on this particular house I am sure no one would object to Mr Larding's palate leading the way.

TRAMPS: – No no certainly not.

– By all means.

– The man has an excellent nose.

Etc., etc.

LARDING is by now the slightest bit pissed.

LARDING: Too kind…

Two of the tramps go over to LIONHEART.

LIONHEART: But soft! Here come my executioners.

To the Tramps.

How now, my hardy, stout, resolved mates!
Are you now going to despatch this thing?

TRAMP 1: We are my lord.

LARDING notices someone dressed as Richard III.

LARDING: What on earth...?

LIONHEART: But, sirs, be sudden in the execution,
Withal obdurate, do not hear him plead;
For Clarence is well spoken, and perhaps
May move your hearts to pity if you mark him.

LARDING: Lionheart, is that you?

TRAMP 2: Tut, tut, my lord! We will not stand to prate;
Talkers are no good doers. Be assured:
We go to use our hands and not our tongues.

LARDING: I really must take my hat off to you. Surviving
that fall. And...and I daresay you're responsible for all
this! (*He indicates everything around him.*) and for
everything that's been happening...most impressive.

*LARDING raises his glass and toasts LIONHEART.
Immediately he is in a reverie.*

Oh Margeaux!

LIONHEART: You disgusting wine bibber! So you slept
through my Richard did you? Because you'd guzzled so
much wine beforehand you snored like a drunken hog
through one of my finest performances.

LARDING: I know, I know. I have a problem, I know. It's
just that... I can't watch any more theatre. Five plays a
week! Can you imagine? Can you? I don't know what
I'm seeing any more... I don't know what to say about
any of it... Oh God Lionheart I know how pathetic I am,
I know how unhappy I am... I can't face it without this.
Those others knew what they were doing every time they
poured scorn on you. Me? Do you know what, do you
know what? My life has been crushed by theatre
criticism just as surely as yours Lionheart. It's my job to
have a reasoned objective judgement on something that
has come from another human being's heart. Good or

bad it has come from their heart. Good or bad it comes
from your heart Lionheart. And I have to sit in
judgement. Pass judgement. Use and explain my
judgement, night after night…

TRAMP 2: The urging of that word judgement hath bred a
kind of remorse in me.

TRAMP 1: What? Art thou afraid?

TRAMP 2: Not to kill him.

LARDING: Imagine what that does to man? Can you? Can
you see how it has destroyed me? made me less than
human?

TRAMP 1: He would insinuate with thee but to make thee
sigh.

TRAMP 2: Tut, I am strong framed; he cannot prevail with
me.

LARDING: When we objectify the subjective we extinguish
its soul. But the soul of the objectifier is extinguished just
as surely as the soul of the subject. The humanity of the
murderer is extinguished just as surely as the life of the
victim. Fate may have put us on different sides
Lionheart, but we are both victims. You and me together.

TRAMP 2: Come shall we fall to work?

LIONHEART: Your eyes drop millstones when fools' eyes
                                        drop tears.
I like you, lads; about your business straight.
Go, go, despatch.

TRAMP 3: We will my noble lord.

TRAMP 4: Throw him in the malmsey-butt.

TRAMP 3: You shall have wine enough my lord anon.

TRAMP 5: Look behind you my lord!

The tramps try to force LARDING head first into the barrel.

LARDING: No! No! Please, I understand you Lionheart. I know what you are going through. Please!

LIONHEART: Unhappy man! Your soul shall be made clean When you are washed to death with fulsome wine.

LARDING is upended into the barrel. His legs kick for a bit and then sink into the wine. The tramps put a lid on the barrel and seal LARDING in.

I thought you might enjoy that Chambertin '64 Larding. It's a vintage that's come on very well. And don't hesitate to complain if it is not sufficiently *chambré.*

The barrel is rolled off stage. All exit.

Scene 15

DEVLIN comes on to the stage carrying a large bundle. It is a piece of sacking wrapped around some things that are clanking noisily.

He dumps the bundle on to the floor. A selection of theatrical weapons and armour spill out.

DEVLIN starts to sort through them. Feeling them in his hand or offering them up to his body to see how they fit.

He puts on a helmet and a breastplate. He chooses a hefty looking battle axe.

MIRANDA enters.

MIRANDA: Nice hat.

DEVLIN: Did you find a way out?

MIRANDA: Doors that were open are locked. Someone wants to keep us here.

DEVLIN: And I know who.

MIRANDA: So you said.

DEVLIN: I saw him. I had a sword fight with him for goodness sake. It's him. It's all him.

MIRANDA: I know.

DEVLIN: You believe me?

MIRANDA: I spoke to him.

DEVLIN: You've seen him?

MIRANDA: On the telephone.

DEVLIN: When?

MIRANDA: Yesterday.

DEVLIN: Yesterday.

MIRANDA: He told me to come here. He said I would see him in his greatest performance. That I would be proud of him. At least I think that's what he said. It was hard to understand – it was all…

DEVLIN: Shakespearean?

MIRANDA: Yea. I mean there was always a sprinkling of quotes; as a sulky teenager I'd get 'How now daughter? What makes this frontlet on? You are too much of late i'the frown.' But yesterday on the phone it was nearly all Shakespeare. It's quite odd hearing Shakespeare on the phone.

There is a moment between them. As if she is finally trying to decide if she can trust DEVLIN.

Peter, I don't want him to be… I couldn't cope with that again.

DEVLIN: Cope with what?

MIRANDA: Him. His…

DEVLIN: What?

MIRANDA: You know how some actors are like children? He was like that, but more. Constantly demanding attention. Constantly demanding to be centre stage. I grew up as the adoring audience, applauding everything he did.

When my mother died, he almost enjoyed it. He revelled in the drama as if it were scene in a play. He never thought to ask if I was alright. My feelings never seemed to matter; his were so big. Whether they were real or acted, I never knew. When I was little I imagined that before he went to bed he peeled off the face he was wearing, and underneath was someone I'd never known. P'haps I was right?

Since he died. Since I thought he was dead. I've had some quiet. I feel like I've been able to look around, at things other than him.

Oh God, listen to me. I don't wish him dead, I just don't want him back.

I don't blame you for what happened.

DEVLIN: Why the change of heart?

MIRANDA: When one's father comes back from the grave as an avenging thespian angel of death – it makes you think about things.

DEVLIN: I suppose it would.

MIRANDA: You were only writing what I wanted to say. 'Wake up!', 'Look at yourself through somebody else's eyes for once.'

DEVLIN: You are nothing like your father.

MIRANDA: That is the nicest thing anyone wearing a bronze breastplate has ever said to me.

We have to stop him.

DEVLIN: I have to stop him.

MIRANDA: I can talk to him.

DEVLIN: There is no way I'm letting him anywhere near you.

MIRANDA: I think he'll listen to me. I remember the way he looked at me in your flat just before he jumped. Somewhere I must mean something to him.

DEVLIN: Whatever we do, we have to find him before he finds us.

MIRANDA: He must be getting ready for another of his 'performances'.

He takes out the poster with the list of plays on.

DEVLIN: We think he's done *The Merchant of Venice.* There were a couple of bits of *Romeo and Juliet* before he appeared with a sword…after that it's *Richard III, Henry VI Part 1, Titus Andronicus* and finally *King Lear.* Plenty of death and destruction there.

MIRANDA: Think about my father. Think what deaths he would choose for theatre critics.

DEVLIN: None of your run of the mill death in a battle scene.

MIRANDA: Something more…

DEVLIN: Sadistic.

MIRANDA: Humiliating.

DEVLIN: *Richard III…*? Princes in the tower, Clarence in the butt of malmsey.

MIRANDA: *Henry VI Part 1…*?

DEVLIN: Terrible play.

MIRANDA: What?

DEVLIN: No one ever does it. Except Lionheart.

MIRANDA: Is that strictly relevant?

DEVLIN: No. Sorry. Joan of Arc.

MIRANDA: What?

DEVLIN: It's about the only memorable bit in the whole turgid thing, they burn Joan of Arc at the stake.

MIRANDA: That'll be it, what's next.

DEVLIN: *Titus Andronicus* – oh Crikey. That could be anything.

MIRANDA realises the significance for her of the last play in the season.

MIRANDA: *King Lear.* The last play. It's *King Lear.*

DEVLIN: Oh God. Miranda… Let's find him and stop him.

They exit.

Scene 16

The truck appears and comes downstage. In the middle of the truck, MOON is now asleep in a hairdresser's chair. She has some rollers in her hair.

LIONHEART is dressed as a trendy and somewhat camp hairdresser. Full Afro wig, big shades, Vegas era Elvis jump suit – the lot.

There is a trolley with some hairdressing paraphernalia on it, which LIONHEART is going through as if preparing for the next stage of a complicated hair treatment.

MOON stirs. She wakes and looks around her. She is confused. She sees LIONHEART (without recognising him) and is alarmed.

LIONHEART: Welcome back to the land of the living duckie. For a while I thought we'd lost you for good.

MOON: Who are you?

LIONHEART: I'm Butch. By name *and* by nature before you ask.

MOON: Butch?

LIONHEART: Hard to believe? I knew I should have ditched the bangles.

MOON: Where am I?

LIONHEART: Don't you recognise it Tinkerbell?

MOON: It looks like Henri's, where I have my hair done.

LIONHEART: Ooh you haven't lost it have you dear.

MOON: But I don't remember coming here, I was in a theatre…

LIONHEART: That'll be the deep scalp massage with pachouli oil. It sent you right off precious. You wouldn't be the first. These fingers can stir up your deepest fears and then wipe the slate clean if you get my meaning.

MOON: Where's Henri?

LIONHEART: Had to go out on a rush job. Princess Margaret needed an emergency perm. Now you stop worrying your pretty head and leave it all up to Butch. You've got dishy dishy hair baby and Butch is doing something special with it.

You are going to be the hottest thing in the West End. Although I wish you'd let me do something camp with the colour darling. I mean like flame with ash highlights.

MOON: These are funny rollers Butch.

She goes to touch them.

LIONHEART: Naughty naughty. Don't touch. Butch knows best. They're something new from gay Paree.

LIONHEART ties her hands to the chair.

MOON: Butch? What are you doing? That's very uncomfortable. I can't move.

LIONHEART reverts to his own voice.

LIONHEART: Behold that sorceress condemned to burn.

MOON: Lionheart! Is that you Edward? What are you doing you wicked man?

LIONHEART produces his scrapbook.

LIONHEART: 'Mr Lionheart is the only actor I have ever seen with stage absence. His performance in *Henry VI Part 1* is so crashingly dull, one suspects he might be taking some kind of personal revenge on the play.'

I think you'll find my new version of the scene where Joan of Arc dies at the stake quite electrifying.

MOON: Don't hurt me. Please. I'll do anything. Anything you want.

LIONHEART: Fell banning hag, enchantress, hold thy tongue.

MOON: Surely you can think of some other way to punish me. Look Edward. I'm all tied up and helpless.

LIONHEART: Thou trull, thou stale, and shameless courtesan!
Dispensing all thy favours only to
Those men that are polluted with your lusts,

MOON: Oh God, oh God!

LIONHEART: Name not religion, for thou lov'st the flesh.

LIONHEART makes the final adjustments to his electrocution equipment.

But I will chastise this high minded strumpet.

See how the ugly witch doth bend her brows
As if, with Circe, she would change my shape.

He pulls the switch. Sparks fly out from the chair and MOON starts to scream and twitch as the electricity flows through the special rollers, into her body.

O burn her, burn her, she hath lived too long,
To fill the world with vicious qualities.

He gradually turns up the current.

Now shine it like a comet of revenge,
A prophet to the fall of all our foes.

LIONHEART turns the current full on. MOON's body is burning.

Foul fiend of flesh and hag of all despite,
Encompassed with thy lustful paramours,

Break thou in pieces and consume to ashes,
Thou foul accursed minister of hell.

Sure that she is dead LIONHEART turns off the current. MOON's body lies motionless but still smoking.

Well Miss Moon, I think you always suspected I was a bit AC/DC. Although you have to admit, I have made you the toast of the town. But I must advise you – this is a no smoking salon.

Scene 17

MIRANDA enters.

DEVLIN appears on the edge of the stage so that he can overhear MIRANDA and LIONHEART, but they cannot see him.

MIRANDA: Father.

I heard her scream.

He looks at MOON's body and realises that his daughter has seen him do this.

LIONHEART: But – O malignant and ill-boding stars –
Now thou art come unto a feast of death.

MIRANDA: Dad…

LIONHEART: I think I have done myself wrong, have I not?

MIRANDA: Dad, stop it.

LIONHEART: My shame and guilt confounds me.

MIRANDA: Stop it! Stop talking like that! This is not a play. You're not acting in a play.

I've seen the things you've done. I want you to be right. I want it to be right but it isn't. Whatever they've done to you…however hateful…

Look what you've done to her.

LIONHEART: Too full of foolish pity is your heart;
Dry up your tears, Miranda. Be collected
There's no harm done.

MIRANDA: Why can't you see!

LIONHEART: No harm.
I have done nothing but in care of thee,
Of thee, my dear one, thee my daughter

MIRANDA: Oh no. Oh no you don't. Don't you start saying you did this for me.

LIONHEART: In former golden days a cherubin
Thou wast that did preserve me. Thou didst smile
As if I did bestride the narrow world
Like a Colossus, but when thou opposed
Thy steadfast-gazing eyes to mine one year

But gone, me thinks I saw it in thy face,
Shame and eternal shame, nothing but shame!
T'was thus Miranda for thine eyes are wounding.

MIRANDA: You selfish, vicious, shit. You've brutally
murdered…I don't know how many people…because I
gave you a bit of a funny look? You've never taken
responsibility for anything. Not me, not Mummy, not
yourself, not your failure. Especially not your
spectacular, dismal, repeated failure.

LIONHEART: Are these things spoken, or do I but dream?

MIRANDA: It was always the critics or the audience or the
other actors or some kind of government conspiracy.

LIONHEART: I prithee, daughter, do not make me mad,

MIRANDA: But it was none of those things, it was you.

LIONHEART: O monstrous! What reproachful words are
these?

MIRANDA: I hate you.

LIONHEART: These words are razors to my wounded heart

MIRANDA: I hate you as a man, I hate you as a father…

LIONHEART: To be so baited, scorned and stormed at

MIRANDA: And I really really hate you as an actor!

You!… Are!… A terrible!… Actor!

LIONHEART: Are you our daughter?

Wilt break my heart?

Ingratitude, thou marble hearted Fiend,

How sharper than a serpent's tooth it is
To have a thankless child. Away, away!

You could have said you didn't like my acting.

MIRANDA: No I couldn't. Look what happened to the people who did.

LIONHEART: Fair point.

MIRANDA: You're going to prison Dad. It's over.

LIONHEART: Yes.

Yes.

Thank God.

He holds out his hands for her to take – she hesitates.

Please Miranda. I know it's not alright. I've done horrible, unforgivable things. I know I've never been much of anything to you and I never will. Not now. But I don't know when I'll hold you again.

She relents, and finds her way, tentatively, into his embrace.

MIRANDA: I'm so glad you stopped before you got to Peter.

He's the only one I talked to.

He was the only one who was kind to me.

LIONHEART: (*Quietly.*) Speak not for him he's a traitor.

MIRANDA: I wasn't speaking for him father he was…he was kind to me.

LIONHEART: Speak not for him.

MIRANDA: Don't tell me what to…

LIONHEART: Silence! One word more
Shall make me chide thee, if not hate thee. What,
An advocate for an impostor?

MIRANDA: But
You have revenge! You have enough revenge!

LIONHEART: No, if I digged up his forefathers' graves
    And hung their rotten coffins up in chains,
    It could not slake mine ire nor ease my heart.

    Urge neither charity nor shame to me.
    Uncharitably with me have you dealt,
    And shamefully my hopes by you are butchered.
    But yet thou art my flesh, my blood, my daughter
    Or rather a disease that's in my flesh,
    Which I must needs call mine. Thou art a boil,
    A plague sore, or embossed carbuncle
    In my corrupted blood… Were't my fitness
    To let these hands obey my blood,
    They are apt enough to dislocate and tear
    Thy flesh and bones.

    LIONHEART grabs hold of her.

    DEVLIN, in armour, carrying his axe steps out onto the stage.

DEVLIN: Lionheart!

    Let her go.

LIONHEART: What sight is this? An armed and angry man?

DEVLIN: I'm not pissing about with you any more.

    DEVLIN begins to move in on LIONHEART, his axe raised.

    LIONHEART grabs a pair of scissors and holds them to MIRANDA's throat.

    DEVLIN stops.

LIONHEART: Hold! Stay thy hand, for doubt not that I will
    Do execution on my flesh and blood.

    DEVLIN and MIRANDA look at each other. LIONHEART notices the look between them.

Ha! Ha! Ha! It goes on, I see.
They have changed eyes. They are both in either's powers.
A pair of star-cross'd lovers. Ha! Ha! Ha!   .

To MIRANDA.

Poor worm thou art infected. Yet, look on.
For ere the glass which now begins to run
Finish the process of this sandy hour,
These eyes that see him now well coloured
Shall see him withered, bloody, pale and dead.

LIONHEART drags MIRANDA away from DEVLIN into the shadows. DEVLIN is left alone.

After a moment we begin to hear a distant noise. Unidentifiable at first, it forms into an approaching war cry that gets louder and louder.

Suddenly, from all directions come soldiers, armed and armoured just like DEVLIN. Flags fly, swords clash and shields crash. All around DEVLIN is an RSC style battle of a seventies vintage. He can't get away. Then all the soldiers turn on DEVLIN.

Just before they finish him off – blackout.

Scene 18

MERRIDEW wanders onto the empty stage. He is looking for his dogs.

MERRIDEW: Cecily…Gwendolen!

O really, this is too much. Where can they be?

How charming of Chloë and Oliver to bugger off and leave me as bait for a sadistic psychopath. Oliver certainly made his feelings about me perfectly clear (although methinks the lady doth protest too much). But, I never thought my babies would run out on their Mama.

Where are you my little darlings?!

Unless the murderer has…no, no I won't let myself think like that. No one could hurt my babies, they're too scrumptious.

Why am I talking to myself?

Some tramps bring on a free standing door. Over the top of the door is an EXIT sign.

MERRIDEW walks up to the door, opens it and looks through. As soon as he does we hear the sound of a busy street and a vibrant street scene comes alive on the other side of the door. It is very theatrical, exaggerated and full of energy and bustle. Although it is not naturalistic, it definitely represents the outside world. There are people walking left and right going about their business.

MERRIDEW closes the door and the street scene stops.

Ah ha! I've found it! The way out!

MERRIDEW clearly believes that the highly theatrical street scene that we have just seen is real.

But what about my darlings? I can't leave them here.

There is the sound of distant trumpets, military drums and cheering men.

VOICE OFF: Romans make way: the good Andronicus,
  Patron of virtue, Rome's best champion,
  Successful in the battles that he fights,
  With honour and with fortune is returned.

A raucous cheer.

MERRIDEW: On the other hand who would look after them if anything happened to me?

MERRIDEW hurries out through the door. Immediately the street scene recommences, just as theatrical as before. MERRIDEW still takes it all to be absolutely real.

The door, with MERRIDEW outside it, turns so that it is now upstage of him, and the street scene is now between us and him.

A cartoonish black cab appears. MERRIDEW hails it.

Taxi!

He climbs in.

Verbena Gardens, Chiswick.

The cab drives off. The journey is all very physical theatre, with props being moved past the cab to simulate movement etc.

CABBIE: Number 22 is it?

MERRIDEW: Yes. How did you know?

CABBIE: S'funniest fing guv'nor. But I saw dees dogs, wanderin' abaht. Little white curly 'aired fings. Frog dogs. You know.

MERRIDEW: Poodles?

CABBIE: Assit. Well I loves animals me and I dint wanna see 'em end up in some char mane. Coz you know wot they's like them chinks, they'll eat anyfink. My bruvver's on the bins right? An' 'e told me...

MERRIDEW: Yes, yes, yes but what about the poodles?

CABBIE: Poodles, yea. Prozzie's dog really innit. You see 'em wiv dem little dogs dontcha? Not that I've ever paid for it mind, never needed to...

MERRIDEW: Please...

CABBIE: Oh yea. Well I stops the sherbet and takes a butchers at the collars and there's a tag says 22 Verbena Gardens. Dint need the Gardens mind, coz vere's only wahn Verbena in the knowledge…

MERRIDEW: The dogs!? What happened to the dogs!?

CABBIE: Oright. Keep yer 'air on. I took 'em to the address and I shoves 'em froo the doggy flap in the back door don't I.

MERRIDEW: You did? O thank you, thank you, thank you.

CABBIE: S'orlright guv'nor. You're lucky they weren't picked up by no mini cab driver, coz they wunt do nuffink for no one.

MERRIDEW: Took a taxi home. Well I never. Oooh I could just eat them up.

A front door with 22 on it is wheeled in. The cab stops outside it.

CABBIE: 'Ere we are guv.

MERRIDEW: Thank you, thank you, thank you again.

He hands a fistful of money to the CABBIE.

Keep the change.

CABBIE: Dunt mind if I do.

MERRIDEW walks through the front door.

MERRIDEW: Cecily! Gwendolen! Mummy's home! Where are my little babies? Come to Mumsie wumsie!

Suddenly we hear a cheesy fanfare that morphs into a TV theme tune, which ends with the words 'This Is Your Dish!' followed by very canned applause.

LIONHEART and COOL DUDE appear, both extravagantly dressed as chefs. LIONHEART has a goatee beard and is carrying his scrapbook as if it is the This Is Your Life *red book. They are surrounded by the tramps who are all being part of a television crew. They have the appropriate props including a couple of very fake looking TV cameras. Some very bright lights are shone at MERRIDEW.*

LIONHEART: Michael Merridew: Theatre critic, gourmand, broadcaster, raconteur, patron of boys clubs and poodle fancier... This Is Your Dish!

Another burst of canned applause.

MERRIDEW: Oh!

Well I never...!

You!

What a divine surprise!

I've often thought how I'd love to be on *This Is Your Dish*, and now that I am I can't think of anything to say except...

Directly into the nearest camera.

This is a very great honour.

Another burst of canned applause. Cameras and lights move around and a chair is brought on for MERRIDEW, who sits behind the table ready to eat a meal which has been placed there.

LIONHEART: The feast is ready!

This is your dish Michael Merridew. It contains your very favourite things and we firmly believe it will prove to be your ultimate meal.

MERRIDEW: It certainly looks very toothsome.

LIONHEART: Will't please you eat? Will't please your highness feed?

MERRIDEW: With pleasure…

Everyone watches intently as MERRIDEW – very much for the camera – takes a mouthful of the food.

After a suitably suspenseful pause.

Simply delicious.

More canned applause.

I can't help wondering where my babies are. My little doggies you know. I think of them as my babies I do love them so.

Sound of a studio audience going 'aaaah'.

'My dish' wouldn't be complete without them.

COOL DUDE wheels on a trolley with a silver domed serving dish on it.

COOL DUDE: I can assure you that your doggies are a very important ingredient in 'Your Dish'.

Big canned laugh.

MERRIDEW: Where are my doggies!

LIONHEART: Why, there they are, both baked in this pie,
Whereof their mother daintily hath fed,
Eating the flesh that she herself hath bred.

MERRIDEW thinks this must be a joke.

MERRIDEW: You had me worried for a minute you naughty man!

LIONHEART: Hark, villain! I did grind their bones to dust
And made a pasty of their shameful heads!

LIONHEART lifts off the dome from the second platter to reveal a pie. Sitting on the top of the pastry are the severed heads of Cecily and Gwendolen.

MERRIDEW: My babies!

LIONHEART takes off his chef's hat and goatee beard.

Lionheart! You swine!

LIONHEART: An appropriate jibe if you remember your description of my Titus Andronicus.

LIONHEART reads from the scrapbook.

'Mr Lionheart's rendering of the role can only be described as villainous. Laid between the delicate performances of Miss Lillywhite as Lavinia and Miss Brown as Tamora, one is irresistibly reminded of a ham sandwich.'

A large table is brought in. At one end is what looks like a big electric mincing machine, with an enormous funnel shaped hopper on the top and a tube coming out of the bottom. MERRIDEW is laid on his back on the table with his head close to this contraption.

MERRIDEW: That was a mistake, a lapse, an aberration. It will never happen again!

LIONHEART: How right you are.

MERRIDEW is strapped to the table. His jaws are forced open and the tube from the bottom of the giant mincer is fed into his mouth and down his throat.

Spoonfuls of the pie are put into the funnel shaped hopper. We see them minced or liquidised, and then we see the resulting gloop travel down the tube into MERRIDEW's mouth.

Thus I enforce thy rotten jaws to open,
And, in despite, I'll cram thee with more food!

More and more of the poodle pie is forced into MERRIDEW, along with the page from LIONHEART's scrapbook with the review on, the poodle heads and anything else that comes to hand.

We can see MERRIDEW's stomach start to distend.

Although the cheer be poor,
'Twill fill your stomach. Please you eat of it.

His stomach is getting bigger and bigger.

Die, frantic wretch, for this accursed deed.

One of the tramps takes a fork and plunges it into MERRIDEW's bloated stomach. There is a loud pop, and the contents of his stomach splatter all over the watching tramps.

Well Mr Merridew; for your last meaI, it looks like you really decided to splash out.

Huge canned laugh and applause followed by the This Is Your Dish *theme tune as all exit and MERRIDEW's body is wheeled away.*

Scene 19

DEVLIN, tied to a chair, is brought on by the tramps.

There is a plinth with a dagger and the Critics' Circle Award on it.

LIONHEART and COOL DUDE enter.

LIONHEART: You were about to announce the winner of the Critics' Circle Award for Shakespeare Mr Devlin. I realise that the rest of your committee are somewhat indisposed, but as chairman you have the casting vote.

DEVLIN does nothing.

Come now Mr Devlin you are holding up the ceremony.

Still DEVLIN does nothing.

Have you dried? It can happen to anyone, allow me to prompt you.

'With this award, we honour a consistently brilliant interpretive artist, and recognise his outstanding contribution to the English theatre as actor and producer. The Critics' Circle Award for Shakespeare goes to…'

DEVLIN: Where's Miranda?

LIONHEART: What?

DEVLIN: Where's your daughter?

LIONHEART: Speak not of her.

DEVLIN: What have you done to your daughter?

LIONHEART: My daughter. My sweet daughter, O. What have I done to you my daughter?

COOL DUDE reveals that he is MIRANDA.

MIRANDA: Good my Lord,
You have begot me, bred me, loved me. I
Return those duties back as are right fit –
Obey you, love you and most honour you.
Give him the award.

DEVLIN: My God Lionheart, you may not be able to act but your daughter certainly can.

MIRANDA: Give him the award!

DEVLIN: No.

LIONHEART: You will recall, Mr Devlin, that the last play in my season was *King Lear*. Remember the fate of Gloucester; blinded to improve his vision of events? Perhaps a similar adjustment will rectify your critical faculties.

DEVLIN: And if I give you the award, I can walk out of here? I don't think so. I'm not going to help you make some sort of sense out of all this by handing you that award. You can kill me Lionheart, but you can't change my mind. William Woodstock won because he brought a thrilling and original perspective to the classical repertoire and you didn't.

LIONHEART: My Julius Caesar, cut down by a mob of derelicts; my electrocuted Joan of Arc; my victorious Shylock; the poodle pie? Was there ever a more original theatrical event?

MIRANDA: And were there not thrills for you in the pursuit of sweet Miranda?

DEVLIN: Why do you care about a critics' award? You think we're idiots, imbeciles. Why do you want our approval?

LIONHEART: Because your approval is the only thing that matters. It is irrelevant what I think of your judgement; your judgement has theatre in its thrall.

DEVLIN: Picasso said that the artist should be aware of the critic in the same way that a bird is aware of the ornithologist.

LIONHEART: But if a species of bird does not meet with the ornithologist's approval does it become extinct?

DEVLIN: Jesus fucking Christ on a bike Lionheart! I've heard all the arguments against us. I've heard them a thousand times. Critics diminish theatre because we record an ephemeral art in permanent ink. Critics' opinions influence the audience response. Critics are divisive, because actors enjoy reading other actors' bad reviews. Critics control the future of theatre because we promote what we like with words and awards and kill off what we don't like with vitriol and indifference. Critics are parasites. Critics are like eunuchs at an orgy… I'm sure you can add to the list, I know I can. We are a very easy target. But without us who do the public turn to? You? If we didn't exist, theatre would have to invent us.

We are quite simply part of the equation. You can kill critics, but you can't kill criticism.

LIONHEART: How refreshing to hear you confess your grip on theatre, but as usual you miss the point. My purpose was not to kill. My purpose was to communicate. This evening has been my gift to you.

DEVLIN: Your gift? You kill four people....

LIONHEART: Six actually, but each of them, with my help, came to understand what it is to have no control over one's own destiny; what it is to live a life utterly under the dominion of others; what it is to be at the mercy of someone who denies responsibility for their power over you; what it is to be an actor. My gift is to help you feel what its like to be me. No…more than that, I want you to understand as I understand.

DEVLIN: Understand what?

LIONHEART: The damage you do. If you only knew. But you must not think I only wish to enlighten critics. There are others. Even more dangerous. And their numbers are growing.

DEVLIN: What others? What the hell are you talking about?

LIONHEART: I have no name for them. I feel them. I can sense them.

DEVLIN: You really are talking like a lunatic. You know that don't you?

LIONHEART: Why should you understand? You are one of them.

DEVLIN: One of what?

LIONHEART: I don't have the words.

DEVLIN: What do they do?

LIONHEART: They don't understand.

DEVLIN: That's what they don't do.

LIONHEART: They... I don't have the words... I can feel it.

DEVLIN: You don't have the words because 'they' don't exist, except in your head as a paranoid excuse for your piss poor productions.

LIONHEART: Why didn't you say anything to poor George Maxwell when he told everyone he'd been offered a job at the new theatre on the South Bank?

DEVLIN: I didn't want to embarrass him.

LIONHEART: That was sweet of you. So your colleagues met their end not knowing that it is you, not George who has been recruited by our new nationalised theatre, as an...erm...?

DEVLIN: Associate Literary Manager.

LIONHEART: Associate Literary Manager. In your office overlooking the river, choosing plays, choosing actors, choosing directors, choosing theatre. Choosing what we see and what we don't see. Establishing an establishment.

DEVLIN: I daresay we'll produce work that challenges the authority of the establishment more than you ever have.

LIONHEART: But will you produce work that challenges the authority of yourselves?

You are part of a new Establishment. Government money flows and suddenly the theatre provides cozy places for university boys; the diplomatic service with artistic knobs on. Magdalene wasn't it? When did you and your kind ever give a damn about the theatre when it had to fend for itself? When it only survived by getting people through the door with the promise of blood or titillation.

But then someone decided that going to the theatre was good for us. Instead of the delicious illicit tang of the betting shop or brothel it had the sanctimonious cultural cache of a collective confessional. Only then, when theatre became a place where careers could be carved? Only then, with establishment sanction did the nice boys move in. Politicians in polo necks who wanted nothing to do with the rough, thrown together, uncontrolled, passionate, instinctive, stinking stuff of acting. Oh no. They won't step on the stage. They want to direct, critique, administrate this ugly chaotic thing. They have the words to explain why that is good and this is not. Everything must be thorough and thought through. Everything must be taken apart and looked at through a microscope to get rid of all the nasty little bugs. Everything must be pasteurized coz pasteurized is best.

DEVLIN: Why not? What's so wrong with thinking something through? What's so wrong with looking at the component parts, in order to improve the whole?

LIONHEART: To create theatre of the highest quality…?

DEVLIN: Yes!

LIONHEART: …and relevance…?

DEVLIN: Yes!

LIONHEART: …and excellence?

DEVLIN: Yes yes yes!

LIONHEART: What has theatre, or sex, or death, or dreams, or pain, or love ever had to do with 'quality' or 'relevance' or 'excellence'?

And now, and now you build a temple to your new, well behaved theatre, a memorial to your triumph over the actor. Will it be run by an actor? Will any actors do the choosing? Oh no. What do actors know about theatre? We are children. It will have nice boys from Oxford and Cambridge who can be trusted to choose wisely and the actors you choose will be so grateful, and never realise that you have stolen theatre from us. Thieved it! Because ever since Thespis stepped forward from the chorus two and a half millennia ago you have wanted to put the spirit back in the bottle. We've been outlawed, stigmatised, ridiculed but nothing worked. The more you disapproved the stronger and more glamorous we became. Until you realised if you can't beat 'em, employ 'em. That's the trick. Domesticate 'em. And on the South bank it will be. A great grey Stalin of a gravestone to actors. It is our death.

Suddenly LIONHEART is in the Lyttelton. He can see the Lyttelton space as we can see it.

Look at it! Look at it! Hard, empty, coy and sexless. Look at it! Smooth and grey so you can wash the blood away when you have done the deed and killed the actor. It should be ours! It should be mine! Brave and foolish, ludicrous and magnificent, wasteful and awesome. Knowing nothing, understanding it all, expressive and inarticulate. We are dead. Murdered like mafia hits and buried in the concrete walls of this mausoleum lest we misbehave, lest something not considered by the brains and the nice boys should spill messily onto the stage. We are the dead.

DEVLIN: Page nineteen. Arts section. The Critics. Last Night's View. *A Theatre of Blood* reviewed by Peter Devlin.

Last night saw the only performance of a fascinating piece of site specific theatre. Radical in its scope and unrivalled in its ferocity, it sets a new benchmark for those that wish to expand the definition of dramatic art.

Questionable on moral and indeed on legal grounds, one cannot question the commitment and planning that must have gone into this production. It is clearly a piece that the originators were burning to perform and it displayed all the urgency and daring that is so often lacking in theatre of this scale.

Although rather episodic, this is a story of revenge, madness and the devotion of a daughter to her father. These are themes that we see time and again in the plays of Shakespeare and themes which run through this piece with a brutal energy that is frightening to behold.

Perhaps the most startling element of this startling production is the emergence of fresh and exciting talent. Miranda Lionheart displays a virtuosity which belies her relative inexperience. She convinces on almost every level, and she handles the many layers of her performance in most attractive style. However, even more of a revelation are the supporting company.

The Tramps respond to being mentioned.

Though this is undoubtedly the first experience of theatre for many, if not all of this rag tag chorus, they embody an earthy strength that has been missing from British theatre for generations. The immediacy and conviction of their every gesture is truly threatening and yet exhilarating.

The Tramps have clearly been affected by the praise.

One would have to say that a great future awaits this ensemble were it not for the millstone that hangs around their collective neck. I refer, alas to the leading player and conceiver of the evening. For this bold and dramatic experiment has at its centre a feeble and hackneyed heart. What a contrast there is between the players I have already described and the tired, posturing of the untutored ham who leads them. To see him perform is to see a horse so dead, so thoroughly flogged that one's first impulse is simply to turn away.

The words seem to drain LIONHEART of his strength. He is like Superman in the presence of Kryptonite.

Mr Lionheart's knowledge of Shakespeare is well known, but in all his reading does he always skip Hamlet's advice to the players? For he speaks no speech trippingly on the tongue. He is the town crier. There is much sawing of the air, passions are torn to tatters and Herod is well and truly out-Heroded.

It is left to Miss Lionheart and the supporting company to suit the action to the word and the word to the action. It is they who hold as t'were a mirror up to nature…

The Tramps are becoming excited and agitated by this. They don't want DEVLIN to stop. They want to hear more about how good they are and how terrible LIONHEART is.

LIONHEART is dazed. In another world. MIRANDA can see what this is doing to him.

MIRANDA: Shut up Devlin.

DEVLIN: …it is thrilling to see such burgeoning talent, but it will never blossom while it is shackled to a player who struts and bellows…

MIRANDA: No more words.

DEVLIN: …as if he had been made by nature's journeymen and not made well…

MIRANDA: I shall cut out your tongue!

DEVLIN: …he imitates humanity so abominably.

MIRANDA grabs the dagger and rushes at DEVLIN.

The Tramps intercept her.

For a moment she is hidden from view.

And then she emerges. She walks towards LIONHEART.

She is covered with blood and she has a bloodied knife in her hands.

MIRANDA: What means this bloody knife? 'Tis hot, it smokes.

LIONHEART holds her in his arms.

How does my royal lord? How fares your majesty?

LIONHEART: You did me wrong to take me out of the grave.

MIRANDA: We are not the first,
Who with best meaning have incurred the worst.
For thee, oppressed king, I am cast down.

She dies.

LIONHEART: Howl, howl, howl! O you are men of stones.
Had I your tongues and eyes, I'd use them so
That heaven's vault should crack. She's gone forever!
I know when one is dead and when one lives,
She's dead as earth. Lend me a looking-glass,
If that her breath will mist or stain the stone,
Why then she lives.

This feather stirs, she lives! If it be so,
It is a chance that does redeem all sorrows
That ever I have felt.

A plague upon you murderers, traitors all!
I might have saved her; now she's gone forever.
Miranda, Miranda, stay a little. Ha?
What is't thou sayst? Her voice was ever soft,
Gentle and low, an excellent thing in woman

Why should a dog, a horse, a rat have life,
And thou no breath at all? Thou'lt come no more,
Never, never, never, never, never.

Pray you undo this button.

                              Thank you sir,
Do you see this? Look on her, look her lips,
Look there, look there!

LIONHEART dies.

*One of the tramps picks up the knife and walks across to
DEVLIN. He pauses for a moment, then cuts DEVLIN free.*

DEVLIN: Come and see me when we move into the
    National. I'm sure we can find some funding for you to
    workshop a few ideas.

DEVLIN exits.

The Tramps exit.

CURTAIN

WWW.OBERONBOOKS.COM

Printed in the USA
CPSIA information can be obtained
at www.ICGtesting.com
LVHW020956171024
794056LV00004B/1172

9 781840 025781